SET FREE FOR OTHERS

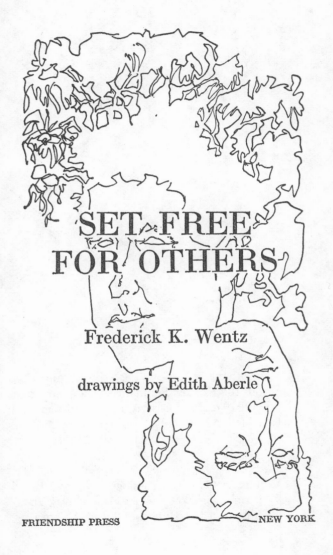

SET FREE
FOR OTHERS

Frederick K. Wentz

drawings by Edith Aberle

FRIENDSHIP PRESS   NEW YORK

Library of Congress Catalogue No. 68-59133
Copyright © 1969 by Friendship Press, Inc.
Printed in the United States of America

To Abdel Ross Wentz
from whom I have learned the most

Contents

Chapter One

Divided Against Ourselves

Reconciliation, one of the central words in Christian experience, means the act of bringing back harmony. Reconciliation implies that there once was harmony, that harmony has been lost and that there is a need for harmony. Furthermore, Christians believe that Jesus Christ is the reconciler, that he brings back the lost harmony —between God and man, between man and his fellowmen, within a man and within the whole universe. We need look no farther than the morning paper to be reminded of the need for reconciliation in American life right now.

Vignettes of Human Division

Our family moved into a new neighborhood recently, a nice suburban community. In the house next door live five girls, who were soon at our door, in our house and close friends with our own youngsters. We have become friends with their parents in an informal, relaxed way. On the other side is a big home that is somewhat removed. The people came out to talk with us on our driveway one day, and now we wave at each other as occasion offers. Our little dog decided to bark vociferously at the lady across the street when she walked her dog. She would shout and swear, and she finally sent police to warn us about creating a disturbance. So our pup is now confined to the backyard. We have learned the names and faces of some of the rest of the neighbors.

All that happened about six months ago. The situation hasn't changed today and may not change as long as we live there—a friendly family, a fractured relationship, some who are neighborly at a distance and some who are simply distant. Eventually we may discover a really lonely couple on our street, maybe some tragic situation, or a rather famous person. But we're probably settled into a fairly typical American, middle-class neighborhood. The relationships are not exciting, but nobody expected them to be more than ordinary.

What really matters is our family of five. For two more years we'll have each other; then one will go away to school and even the family will change. Already communication is becoming difficult between adolescents and their parents.

We have our friends at work, at three schools, at our many clubs and voluntary societies, our congregation. And there are many potential friends in the small university community to which we belong. Some few of them we'll learn to cherish; many more we'll hope to cultivate in future months. Yet in the seventeen years that we've been married we have moved four times; we hardly expect anymore to develop close and abiding friendships.

We're just terribly busy. We move too fast. We're caught up in many activities, in as many different involvements. We really have no opportunity to learn to know anybody well. Except maybe husband and wife.

Is this your story too? Do you know anybody really well? Actually, how many deep, abiding relationships are there in our modern civilization?

In Edward Albee's *Zoo Story* a man is reading his newspaper in the park, minding his own business, when he is interrupted by another man. Newspaper poised, he remains polite for a while but then becomes annoyed at the interference, especially because the second man pours out his troubles in a way that threatens to involve the man on the park bench. As the intruder persists he succeeds in getting the first man angry. In the ensuing scuffle the intruder successfully maneuvers the first man into stabbing him fatally. Then, as he lies dying, he expresses to the horrified assailant his satisfaction at having finally related himself in a significant way to another human being. So desperate is the human condition, Albee seems to be saying. So sadly are we unconnected with each other. So dire is our loneliness.

There are plenty of people, of course, and plenty of contacts. The modern city has been compared to a giant switchboard that exists to make many connections. People moving on the streets, men in offices telephoning and meeting in conferences, advertisements and radio-TV programs, buses and subways and airplanes and endless lines of cars—all making a multitude of human contacts.

Yet how many of these produce significant human encounters? When thousands of people are thrown together in a city they learn to ignore each other and develop a sense of distance. The distance is there not only when a disreputable figure stumbles and falls into the gutter on a busy street; not only when a woman is murdered at night and her screams bring neighbors to peek out their windows, but not to help. The distance is also there when neighbors rub shoulders in the elevator or wave to each other from across the street. Seeking to bring the church into the huge circular towers of Marina City in Chicago, a pastor moved his family into one of the apartments.

After two weeks in Marina City I was still unsure about how to meet its people. One day I found myself an elevator passenger with two young women. I reached for the 45th-floor button, and so did they. Here was my

chance. With typical suburban-pastor friend-
liness I said, "We must live on the same
floor."

No answer. They seemed to respond with
a "What's with him?" kind of glance. They
were not irritated, but they made no effort to
reply.

We left the elevator at the 45th floor and
headed down the corridor. As I reached for
my doorknob, they reached for theirs six
inches away. Again my suburban-pastor mind
drew a brilliant conclusion, and I exclaimed
happily, "We must live right next to each
other."

At this there was an audible sigh, a condescending "somebody's going to have to say
something" response, "Well, welcome to
Marina City." [1]

Unconnected people easily become suspicious
of one another. Charles Lamb is said to have
commented to a friend as another man passed:
"There goes a man I hate." His friend exclaimed
in surprise: "I didn't realize you even knew that
fellow." "I don't," replied Lamb, "that's why
I hate him." Small differences, a bit of strange
expression or action, readily become the basis for
distrust and rejection.

Barriers Between Us

Conflict is another of the ingredients of life
that are common to us all. When we do actually
connect with other people we run into opposi-

[1] Footnotes begin on page 156.

tion and hostility. Because people are different, when they rub together their divergent interests and purposes produce friction and sparks. Prolonged and violent encounter may engender hatred. More steady are the little irritations built into the relationships that are given us each day. Here is the teacher whose condescending attitude spreads misery in the school, the secretary whose bumbling stems from her lackadaisical approach to her tasks, the aging friend who talks endlessly and boringly about her aches and pains and about the people she doesn't like. Some people seem to be walking sore thumbs. One housewife tells of this incident:

> Ahead of me in a line at the supermarket was a large woman, securely wrapped in her fur coat and mad at the world. In whining complaint, she started in on the hapless checker. There was a bottle missing from her carton of soft drink and she wouldn't pay for it; this was the beginning of a tirade against the store, the soft drink company, and the size of bottles. It looked like a long wait, and I gave my four-year-old a penny for the bubble gum machine.

> The woman advanced to questioning each amount on her register slip. Finally she picked up her bag of groceries to depart—just as my small son returned. They bumped just hard enough to jostle her groceries, and pickle juice began to drip down on the counter.

> "He tripped me," she said in a piercing voice. "That child tripped me!" And she was

launched again on a loud and long recital
about that awful child, his irresponsible parents, awful children in general—and who was
going to pay for the pickles.[2]

Social conflicts carry much more dynamite
than our private feuds and our personal irritations. All of us are caught in the swirl of social
passions in the twentieth century. Stokely Car-
michael used these words about black vengeance:

> We are not waiting for them to kill us.
> We will move to kill them first, or rather, we
> are working towards that goal. . . . One good
> thing about the Vietnam war is that the
> United States has taught us how to kill. Our
> brothers returning from Vietnam are going
> to use that training well in the cities of the
> United States.[3]

Referring to the "legacy of barriers" that sepa-
rates blacks and whites in Africa, L. Arden
Almquist, in an article entitled "Whitey Your
Time Is Running Out," describes a scene from
his missionary experiences:

> It is mid-morning. A Portuguese trader
> arrives at the mission with an aching tooth.
> I am expected to leave the Africans waiting to
> see me at the hospital and tend to him. Hav-
> ing just had an operation on my hand and not
> yet having recovered the strength of my
> grip, I take the precaution in my naiveté to
> ask the African nurse who is my right-hand
> man to come along and help. After several
> futile attemps to dislodge the tooth, I turn

15

to Nutumbo and say: "Here, you try." He
hesitates a moment—long schooled in the
way of the Portuguese—but accepts the
instrument. The white man closes his jaw
firmly, shakes his head and says, "Not him!
Never! You do it." [4]

All over the world men have created fences,
trade barriers, legal segregations, exclusive clubs,
restricted neighborhoods. They have dropped
massive Iron and Bamboo Curtains. In 1961 the
Communist East Germans erected their famous
wall between East and West Berlin, separating
friends, parents and children, business associates,
fellow townsmen.

These deep social cleavages divide our home-
towns as well. As one Cleveland woman put it:
"The world's battlelines run right through the
heart of Cleveland." Indeed, they are echoed
within every human heart in one form or another.

Not many homes escape some experience with
the generation gap. Teen-agers start to feel for
their own independence and to test their changing relation to their parents, teachers and other
authorities in their lives. At the same time they
embrace passionately a subculture of their own,
which strikes their elders as either a complete
mystery or shockingly irresponsible. Speaking of
college students who commute, Roy Enquist
points out that they

    . . . usually live at home with parents,
    most of whom have not themselves had col-

lege experience. The family tends to regard the commuter student as simply continuing his high school training. The determined efforts of the college to effect a change in the mentality and competence of its students is usually feared and resented by the family; each evening two different, irreconcilable worlds meet face to face.[5]

There are many other thought worlds which, when we inhabit them, divide us from our fellows. Even at family gatherings it is often unwise to discuss politics because deep-laid and irreconcilable viewpoints will emerge and provoke hostilities. Or Martin Luther King should not be mentioned lest tempers flare. A person who talks of fair housing in his immediate neighborhood suddenly finds that some of his acquaintances live in one world of thought and others breathe an entirely different mental air.

The Threat of Meaninglessness

On a larger scale we find a great chasm between those in our society who despair of mankind and those who are wildly hopeful of a breakthrough into a better world. Many people find life deeply meaningless. For them God is dead; all real authority has collapsed; what is there to lay hold of? They can only wait, caught in a slum or a daily rat race, tied up in a machine or a corporation or a marriage that is alternately bitter and dull. Marilyn Haney caught that mood in a few lines:

The thermos bottle
smiled condescendingly
at the little man,
for its vacuum
had a purpose.[6]

On the other hand, there are those who are almost messianically sure they know the meaning of modern life—Chinese Communists, leaders of new African nations and new civil rights movements, self-confident advocates of the Great Society. Above all, there are the scientists and technologists, some of whom are marching into the future with new formulas that proclaim the wholesale rebirth of humanity and environment —by travel to distant planets, by control of the genes, by the restructuring of our moral habits.

Even more tragic is the separation between the haves and the have-nots. Between nations choked with affluence and peoples tugging at their bootstraps to raise themselves from tribal life into the twentieth century, mostly with their bare hands and their fierce desires. Between the plush security of many of our suburbs and the grinding syndrome of debt, disease, ignorance and despair that raises its stench in the slums.

Recently I heard a radio commentator declare that we should keep a little poverty around so that modern youngsters will develop initiative. I trust that he will keep his own children a little poor, eating slightly unbalanced meals, living in a somewhat run-down neighborhood with substandard hospitals and inadequate schools, and will vacation with them at slightly trashy resorts so they will develop the proper attitudes. It's easy for people who are comfortably situated to register their concern for the national debt in terms of a reduction of welfare programs. Until they have carefully translated this action into the actual experience of a mother whose husband has deserted her, as she struggles to raise a family on the meager allowances for food and clothing that welfare programs provide, they do not realize how their vote for reduced welfare moneys raises bleak barriers and fosters a despair that readily becomes bitter hostility. The affluent and the poverty-stricken live in the same town; they inhabit entirely different worlds.

A pastor of an inner city church in Brooklyn included these paragraphs in his Christmas letter to his people:

> He was eight months old and very sick. The mother took him to the clinic and they kept her waiting four hours before they saw her. But he was already dead by then. . . . The schools are more segregated this year. The brighter children are only two years behind by seventh grade. By ninth grade one in ten will still have a chance to go to college. And parents will still try to believe that their children are being educated. Merry Christmass!

> She was beaten again last night. But she will cover the marks with her long-sleeve sweater and she will smile. And she won't say anything because she wants to keep her

man. She only prays that he will not hurt the
kids. . . . He is well-fed and a big leader
of Christian laymen. He tells me he is sick
and tired of all these sob stories about the
inner-city. He says "those people" can get
ahead just like he did if they only try. He
even has a couple of "them" working for
him and he gets along just fine with them.
Merry Christmass! [7]

Our daily lives are studded with barriers,
though they are often invisible and the separations they cause are often unconscious. Our society bears the scars and the deep wounds of many
cleavages, though we may stay among our own
kind and not be aware of the gulfs that yawn
between groups of men.

Glimpses of Brotherhood

Is this the human condition? Or are we simply
a particularly nasty nest of humankind? Is it
urban man that is caught in these webs? Or
Western man, or civilized man, or technological
man, or secular man, or twentieth century man?
Or is it really man, himself and as he actually
is, who experiences frustrating limits, ghettoed
separations, conflicts and enmities?

This is not, of course, the *whole* human condition. One can quickly catalog human ties that
do bind and often bless—family and nation,
common occupation or leisure interest, neighborhood associations and political affiliations, the
congregation or the country club or the school,

21

common endeavors such as the Community Chest or a society for more humane abortion laws.

At times one knows that he has been blessed by such ties. An alumnus sees his son graduate from his own alma mater. The "Star-Spangled Banner" is played before a football game while thousands pause. The oldest daughter's sixteenth birthday portends change in the family circle. The funeral of a patriarch brings the clan together to reminisce about days long gone. A political party celebrates its victory. A faithful employee is honored at the time of retirement.

Each of these bonds limits and excludes at the same time that it unites and strengthens. Only rarely are there breakthroughs that go beyond clan and nation to suggest a common humanity. An exchange student lives in an American home. A black African touches chords of response in a white American audience. A well-educated lawyer lives in the slums of Harlem, offering both legal advice and human counsel to a steady stream of disadvantaged and bewildered blacks and Puerto Ricans. The Red Cross carries through an act of mercy that penetrates a battle line. Missionaries and Peace Corp Volunteers painfully identify with primitive peoples in remote spots. Let one more scene from "Whitey Your Time Is Running Out" serve as illustration:

> There is a strike at the Wasolo station. It began with the dismissal of some student nurses. Soon the solidarity of the African

community manifests itself. The workmen quit working and all building ceases. The school teachers send the two hundred pupils home. It is my fault—I had injured the Africans' keen sense of justice in a gesture of anger. The senior missionary on the station tells me: "This is your problem. You handle it." Humbled after thoughtful praying, I take a can of powdered coffee and some sacks of sugar and go to the African village down the hill where the strikers, in a sullen mood, are sitting around. I tell them I am sorry, ask them to add hot water to the symbols of reconciliation in my hands, and invite them to share a cup of coffee with me and talk things over. There are murmurs of surprise, and suddenly there is joy. We drink together and are friends again. Then someone says, "You are the first white man who ever apologized to us." [8]

Yet experiences that clearly proclaim a common humanity uniting the whole human race are brief and fleeting. They are also rare and precious. Most of us believe in the brotherhood of man, but our experience of it is vague—a few glimpses, some yearnings, an occasional sign in an unusual happening. Most of the solid associations within which we live are limited. And, as we have seen, even these bonds are often severed, or exclusive enough to engender conflict. The human condition, as we vividly experience it, includes frustrating limits, ghettoed separations, conflicts and hostilities, as well as glimmerings of something more broad and more complete.

What is the human condition? What is man? What kind of relationships really belong to human life? How shall we interpret these experiences?

Chapter Two

What Is Man?

$\mathbb{T}$oday we are besieged by many images of man, images that compete and often conflict. How we view a man and mankind determines what we see in human relationships and what we expect of them.

Each ideology among us, each advertiser, promotes some picture of what a real man is—he drinks with distinction; he has drive; his body ripples with muscles; he buys United States bonds; he needs a yacht for the full life.

"What a Great Boy Am I!"

Even nursery rhymes carry images of man. Jack Horner, for example, reflects attitudes that have become typical of secularist America. You remember it goes like this:

Little Jack Horner sat in a corner,
Eating his Christmas pie.
He put in his thumb
And pulled out a plum,
And said, What a great boy am I!

Here God provided the rain and the sun; some farmer had to raise the fruit and produce the flour for the pie; Jack's father toiled hard to be able to buy the ingredients; his mother baked it and served it. All Jack did was to stick in his thumb—no very creditable activity—yet his conclusion was, "What a great boy am I!" Little Jack *felt* like a great boy, so he said he was one.

This rhyme is a kind of parable of modern, secular, democratic society. We do not exactly say, "What a great boy am I!"; we say we believe as one of our democratic principles in the dignity and worth of human personality, the importance of the individual. We talk a lot about it, because that principle is necessary to our thinking in Western civilization. But it is mostly talk; we have nothing to back it up. When we say every individual is important, that is just the way we feel. What arguments, what proof can a secular society produce today? Our position is not much better than a boasting Jack Horner, sitting there with a plum stuck on his thumb.

It's the old question, you see, that the Psalmist asked centuries ago when he wrote the eighth Psalm: "What is man?" People in modern Western civilization are far too prone to respond brightly, "That's a very good question; I'm glad that you asked it." But they cannot answer it. Or they have myriad answers and each field of knowledge adds a different one. Yet this question is a crucial issue in the earth-shaking struggle of the Western democracies with communism. The Communists don't believe in the importance of the individual; each man is tiny and unimportant before the great superstate or supersociety. On the other hand, Communists consider men good, so good that taken in the mass they will build up that superstate eagerly when they have been freed from capitalism and classes.

The founders of the United States, while having faith in the people, had a more accurate appraisal of human goodness. Human relationships are easily distorted or fractured. When James Madison and the writers of the Constitution put a careful system of checks and balances into our representative government, they were acting as political realists, who recognized that men are not entirely trustworthy but have some predatory characteristics. This realism can be traced back to the Reformation and to the Judeo-Christian tradition and the biblical view of God and man.

But now what about that other point, the bigness of man, the importance of the individual? That was a still greater part of the faith of the founding fathers. In fact they built their theory of democracy and their democratic nation upon it—the inalienable rights of men as men. Here too the idea goes back to the Reformation and the Judeo-Christian tradition.

We believe this today too, but there is a difference. The founding fathers knew *why* they believed in the dignity of man. They could give reasons, which were based on their other beliefs. Modern Western civilization has only inherited it from them and just *feels* that way about it, in Jack Horner fashion. As eighteenth century Christians, rationalists and deists, they believed in God who had created the universe and made man, made him a marvelous, valuable creature with an immortal soul, destined for God's heaven. They believed in reason and thought man's mind was a precious endowment that could think true thoughts and guide rational actions. They believed in a natural law, instituted by God and establishing across the world the inviolable consciences of men who must then treat other men as brothers. That is where the democratic principle of the importance of the individual was nurtured.

Today, however, that subsoil is gone, eroded by many winds and rains over the years. Astronomers have told us of the hugeness of the universe with its galaxies upon galaxies of stars and the possibility of a hundred million earths like ours, until man seems but a tiny occurrence in a remote corner of the universe. Geologists point out that if the age of the earth were the height of the Empire State Building, the story of human existence would have the thickness of a book perched on top of the tower, and recorded history would be a thin dime laid upon the book.

Evolutionists have stressed our kinship with the higher animals, making mankind a mutation in the monkey family. Freudian psychologists picture man as a battleground for the id, the ego and the superego, his freedom purely illusion since his subconscious controls him, and his mind and its thoughts the effervescent froth thrown off by his underlying emotions. Sociologists see us as the products of our physical and cultural environment, our morals relative to time and place, our beliefs really only outmoded customs that we can discard in the name of freedom. Even some philosophers stress that ideas are instruments to be held only so long as they help people make satisfactory adjustments in life.

As a crowning insult we learn that our vaunted civilization has produced a generation of synthetic barbarians, mass men, crowds of people who have no culture or faith, whose inner emptiness makes them far more destructive than any primitive tribesmen. Contemporary events do not make man seem important or give the individual much value. The Nazis tried to "exterminate" (a term formerly applied to rats) six million Jews; the Communists can take a person apart and reconstruct him to fit their wishes for a public trial. One University of Chicago medical man, after describing how physicians with the help of drugs can slow up bodily processes, control moods and deaden pain, said: "Man may appear in some respects to have become a compliant bit of putty in the hands of the physician."

Even our end appears ignominious today—a bomb will drop on some important objective miles away and we shall burn and suffocate in the dust that arises.

No, man is not very big, viewed by contemporary thought and events, and when men of the modern West assert his great worth, they assert only a feeble feeling.

Without trust in God, the secular American has no basis for reverencing the individual and nurturing his life.

Mindful of Man

The answer to the question, "What is man?" comes right only as we look away from man and look at God. The Psalmist was not really asking, "What is man?" He was asking, "What is man that *thou* [God] art mindful of him and the son of man that *thou* dost care for him?" This is a song of praise to God. It starts, "O Lord, our Lord, how majestic is thy name in all the earth!" And it ends with the same refrain. That is the right context for a proper understanding of a human being. Against that background, within that frame, we come to see more clearly.

In other words, *a man is to be understood primarily by his relationships, and his crucial relationship is with God.*

Psalm 8 helps us to see even more about man. In himself, apart from God, man is not much; indeed, he is puny and miserable and unimportant.

When I look at thy heavens, the work
of thy fingers,
the moon and the stars which
thou hast established;
what is man that thou art mindful
of him,
and the son of man that thou
dost care for him?

We would have to admit that there are many scientific truths behind the deflating generalizations we just attributed to geologists and Freudians and sociologists. Yet God *is* mindful of men. God crowns man with glory and gives him dominion.

Yet thou hast made him little less
than God,
and dost crown him with glory
and honor.
Thou hast given him dominion over
the works of thy hands;
thou hast put all things under his
feet, . . .

Man is created by God. He is the peak of creation because God made him the peak and gave him dominion. His value and his place on earth stem from his relation to God.

With the help of the whole biblical revelation and in the light of Jesus Christ himself, we have a number of further clues about what a man is. From the perspective of Christ, man takes on two new dimensions. The first is a vertical dimension that illuminates both man's stature, or height, and his degradation, or depth. The second dimension is that of time, or history.

But before turning to man's vertical dimension as a spirit, we must first emphasize that he *is* embedded in nature and fully a part of the natural world. Man not only *has* a body; he *is* a body. Certainly he is not a soulless physique, but neither is he a disembodied spirit. From the biblical viewpoint, he is not so much an embodied soul as he is an ensouled body (Genesis 2:7). The Apostles' Creed symbolizes this emphasis by its reference to the resurrection of that body in the hereafter. In this life, that body participates fully in the material world, in the flux and cycles of nature, in growth and decay, full participation in the vicissitudes, the wear and tear, the accidental invasions, the parasites, as well as the glow and beauty and energy of the whole round of natural life.

Furthermore, it is *good* that man should be a part of nature. God made the material and biological world. He made man an integral part of it. And he saw that it was all good, as we are told repeatedly in the first chapter of Genesis.

For the Christian, however, the Incarnation (enfleshment) indicates still more convincingly that man's part in the material world is good. Jesus Christ, the Son of God himself, came into this world, became fully man and fully flesh, entering into all the limitations of earthly existence. By that action, he hallowed the human round.

The Vertical Dimension

Now, however, it is a crucial part of Christian revelation that man has a stature, a vertical dimension, which rises above the rest of nature. He has been made a "little less than God." That is, he is *spirit* as well as body. Or better, since spirit is a vague word, *man is made in the image of God* (Genesis 1:26–27). This means at least three things.

Man is a *person*, that is, he is free and responsible. Though he is strictly limited by his setting in time, place, heredity and environment, man is nonetheless free to make choices. He can to some extent modify his environment and shape his course. He can accept or revolt against his intended destiny and thereby exercise the power of self-determination. The man who revolts against his destiny is a different person from the one who accepts his destiny. No other creature has such power—a pig cannot rebel against swinishness, nor can he actively accept his role as a pig. Beyond all else in nature, man is free.

At the same time man is a self, conscious of himself, conscious of a history of the self with memory and continuity, capable of being addressed by other persons, shaped by his dialogue with other selves. In other words, he is *responsible*, able to respond and to bind himself in promises, responsible for his actions, willing to take credit or blame for them. At least this much it means to be a person.

33

But now this self or person, grounded in the natural world, is open and free in his highest reaches. This is the second thing meant by "image of God": man is *open upward*. Man is self-transcending, with no limits within himself. There is a quality of the human spirit which, in Reinhold Niebuhr's words, is able "to lift itself above itself as living organism and to make the whole temporal and spatial world, including itself, the object of its knowledge." [1] His spirit reaches even beyond his rational capacity to understand his universe. There is no end to this self-transcendence because the self can always rise above to observe itself observing. Here is a soaring spirit with endless potentialities.

What is man? We do not know until we know God. As Niebuhr puts it, "man is a creature who cannot find a true norm short of the nature of ultimate reality." [2] We do not know ourselves until we know ourselves in God.

The image of God means, then, that man is shaped for a higher life, for fellowship with God. Man has the possibility of an everlasting life of love with a heavenly Father. Our fulfilment and completion are in him alone. Our souls are restless until they find their rest in God. Without an active fellowship with God, man is incomplete, disordered, insecure.

In other words, in God is to be found the rounding off of our humanity. This is true not only in the sense that it is in God we discover the peak of man's vertical dimension. It is also

true in the sense that before God man's true limits are set. Though we are the peak of creation we are yet finite creatures, quite other than the infinite Creator. Thus are we given distinct boundaries for our spirits as well as our bodies. It is our glory that we are capable of fellowship with him; it is our humble necessity to accept our utter dependence upon him.

In yet a third sense is the rounding off of our humanity to be discovered in God. He integrates us, makes us whole. It is God's gift that a man is not a collection of parts or simply a piece of his environment. And each unit finds its completion in being integrated into a larger universe, whose unity consists of a common source, center and sovereign, God. A complete man, then, is one whose natural body and transcending spirit are a harmonious unity, harmoniously related to the environment of things and persons, and in perfectly dependent fellowship with God. This is wholeness and full health. This is man as God made him, according to the Christian understanding.

The Horizontal Dimension

Yet such a picture of man's nature cannot be the whole story. Men do not experience unbroken harmony. Discord is an equally vivid part of human experience. How can this be? Many hypotheses have been proposed, and one interpretation has predominated among those who turn to the Bible for answers to such basic questions.

From the biblical perspective, the Christian theologian adds a second dimension to man's nature. It is the *horizontal* dimension of *passage through time.* Again there are two directions: past and future. Man has a history and he has a destiny. Moreover, when we look back at man's history we discover there the second direction of man's vertical dimension, *depth.*

One of the finest gifts God gave to this peak of his creation was the gift of freedom, the power of choice. In making creatures after his own image, God created the *possibility* of wrong choice and of the entrance of evil into his universe. But the wrong exercise of the power of choice, the actual introduction of evil, was an act in history by a man. At the beginning of history, through no fault in the freedom God had given, man refused his intended destiny, sought to transgress his limits and, in fact, added a new dimension to his nature. This was man denying his own nature, refusing his place in the universe as a dependent creature bearing the image of the Creator. This was rebellion against God, cutting off from him, denying dependence on him and defacing the divine image in man.

Now, therefore, either a man tries proudly to usurp God's place as the infinite center of the universe or tries to reduce himself to the natural world, claiming in a sense that the life of a pig or a wolf represents the essence of humanity. In either case, man actually degrades himself. So universal and all-pervading is this condition that it can be considered a part of man's nature, as the face stamped on the penny is part of the penny. Man has great value and potential before God, but he is also used to twisting his potential toward ends that are ultimately self-defeating. As Reinhold Neibuhr has put it: "Christianity measures the stature of man more highly and his virtue more severely than any alternative view." [3]

And, indeed, the annals of recorded human history do picture just such a fractured, discordant, self-defeating human existence. History also shows, of course, many human accomplishments and many noble human actions. Neither image of man can be proven decisive by an analysis of history. In the early decades of the twentieth century, many of society's leaders thought that history was a record of human progress and that men were increasing their ability to relate harmoniously to one another. Today the idea of steady or overall progress in human history is largely rejected. There is discernible progress in particular fields of endeavor, for example, in scientific investigation and in technology; there are ups and downs in most aspects of human experience. But if any overall progress can be seen in human affairs, it is in the growth of opportunities for choice, in the increase of the number of people who are faced with the necessity of deciding for good or evil. Even such a limited acceptance of the idea of progress does not emerge so much from a careful study of history as from the biblical interpretation of history, in

38

which both good and evil grow until God puts an end to the human procession.

Much of our great literature joins the biblical perspective and the fragmentary lessons of history to describe the human situation as disjointed and less than idyllic. Shakespeare, for example, has portrayed with great power the workings of guilt in the human breast. Not many of us commit cold-blooded murder as did Lady Macbeth, but nearly every one of us knows enough about guilt to live himself into the rest of the heroine's experience in that play. We can feel the clinging, tenacious, deeply embedded hold of guilt upon us. For Lady Macbeth, the spot of blood on her hand was an indelible stain. To the very end of the play we can see her scrubbing piteously at it, crying: "Out, damned spot! out, I say!" While her husband pleads with the physician:

> Cure her of that.
> Canst thou not minister to a mind diseased,
> Pluck from the memory a rooted sorrow,
> Raze out the written troubles of the brain,
> And with some sweet oblivious antidote
> Cleanse the stuff'd bosom of that perilous stuff
> Which weighs upon the heart?

And of course the answer is no. Neither her husband nor a doctor can help Lady Macbeth, because she has let her guilt feelings get out of control. We can only sympathize out of our own guilt feelings.

We have felt the weight and sensed the peril of guilt in our own lives. There are those among us who become obsessed with the sense of guilt, let it paralyze them and get them down. They may jump into a hasty suicide as did Judas in reacting to Christ's crucifixion, or go insane as did Lady Macbeth. Most of us carry a tremendous psychic burden even in leading "normal" lives.

Guilt and Modern Man

Yet perhaps more typical of our contemporary mood is the effort to get rid of guilt feelings. It is plain that there are some in our modern society who have managed to do so—from those whose police dogs snap at peaceful demonstrators, to Communist armies overrunning an obstreperous ally, to those who ride their commuter trains through the heart of the inner city without ever seeing the misery they bisect each day. But the trend toward divesting ourselves of guilt is perhaps best evidenced by the popularity and prestige of psychoanalysts. They have been termed the high priests of modern man. In the popular mind (and this is not a criticism of psychoanalysts, but an interpretation of their popularity), they function as experts in ridding people of a guilty conscience by a Pilate-like ritual of mind washing. Their prestige indicates that our society is aware of psychological distortion and nagged by a sense of guilt.

Here again Christian perspectives sharpen the image. Men are not only guilty of specific misdeeds and possessed of free-swinging, vague guilt feelings with no proper object; men are guilty in a basic way and *should* have guilt feelings because they have rebelled and live in defiance of their Creator.

Modern literary spokesmen tend to depict the threat in terms of meaninglessness rather than guilt. The classic example is Samuel Beckett's play, *Waiting for Godot*. Its actors are largely action-less, waiting. Along the road come bypassers providing trivial incidents, but throughout several acts the two main characters wait for something or somebody. They are not sure what or who; they are not sure he will come. But wait they must, for otherwise their lives are meaningless. This is the situation of modern man. He waits for someone or some event to bring meaning into his existence. Meanwhile he is anxious—afraid of meaninglessness. He may be wistful—"Oh that I could believe these Communists or these Christians with their excited convictions." He knows he is incomplete, but he can only wait for something unknown to complete him.

Actually this is the human dilemma in any age. In New Testament times men were multiplying gods, trying vainly to fill a spiritual vacuum. In the nineteenth century the poet Wordsworth wrote about "Intimations of Immortality"—not so much proving immortality as evidencing the human yearning for it. "You just can't squeeze reality into the span between two dates on a tombstone," says Paul Scherer, and Rufus Jones adds, "Our greatest objective in life is to find the rest of ourselves."

41

Biblical perspectives, fragments of history, literary interpreters; to these images of man one can add the analysts of the social scene today and the prophesying of our sociologists. There are some bold optimists, but most of the watchmen are sounding somber warnings. The portrait is that of frustrated, defeated individuals overwhelmed by massive, impersonal forces that seem to dominate the universe. They face a population explosion around the world, the clash and tensions between competing ideological systems, globeshaking bombs, obliteration warfare, interstellar missiles, an economy of abundance and automation and a proliferation of impersonal bureaucracies in every area of common life. How can a man accomplish anything for himself? He becomes a fatalist who sees himself doomed to be a faceless unit in the lonely crowd, inevitably a status seeker or a mass man, part of a herd of sheep tended by an omnicompetent technology and regularly fleeced by an all-pervasive subliminal advertising.

Once more Christianity can add perspective. Behind social forces and the processes of nature there is a struggle of wills in the universe. Though God governs, there is civil war among the elemental spirits, and that not only in the human ego. There are superhuman evil spirits, demonic forces. Men have allowed their wills to be taken captive not only by sin and death but also by the devil, or at least by the superhuman demonic powers that hold men in slavery, frustrating man's intended destiny with God.

Beset by guilt, waiting in meaninglessness, threatened by frustrating defeat—these could be summed up in the word, "anxious." Ours is the anxious generation. We do not know whether we are gods or beasts. We are insecure, unbalanced, torn, diseased, because we have lost the wholeness that was ours at creation. We are unintegrated. Body and spirit are at odds. The cycles of the body defeat the spirit, and the warped spirit rends the flesh, because they are not united as part of a larger harmony. Men have misused nature, thinking themselves lords instead of stewards of creation. Seeking selfishly to manipulate one another, men have lost their personhood in a depersonalized society. And all because men do not know God aright and are in discordant, grinding relationship to their ultimate Creator and Sovereign. "Wretched man that I am! Who will deliver me from this body of death?" (Romans 7:24). Men need reconciliation.

Fortunately, this is not the whole story of man. Created in the image of God and himself distorting that image, he is yet given a new destiny. Though he has himself frustrated any fulfilment of the loving relationships that were his birthright, which he even now dimly experiences, there is hope for him. In the next breath after Paul had called himself a wretched man he added: "Thanks be to God through Jesus Christ our Lord!" To creation and sin must be added a third segment of the story—reconciliation.

Chapter Three

God So Loves

Man has a future, a destiny; at the least he has a hope. Strangely enough, it comes to him out of the past and is embedded in several thousand years of tradition—yet it is ever-fresh good news. It is the gospel! God not only makes men, but as they strike off on their own, he recovers them and remakes them. The gospel, the good news, is that God is reconciling, bringing harmony again, bringing back friendship.

How can these things be? This is the question Nicodemus asked when Jesus announced that a man must be born anew if he would see the kingdom of God. "How can a man be born when he is old? Can he enter a second time into his mother's womb and be born?" (John 3:4)

What Jesus was saying was just that startling.

Yet Christians have been experiencing it for 2,000 years. It is a mystery, something amazing that God does and men announce as good news. And men find the best explanation in the one Jesus gave to Nicodemus: "For God so loved the world that he gave his only Son, that whoever believes in him should not perish but have eternal life" (John 3:16). Or as Paul stated it: "God was in Christ reconciling the world to himself" (2 Corinthians 5:19).

Is it new life or is it renewed friendship? Both! And much more. We can only express man's destiny in human terms, in analogy with the other experiences of men. The New Testament uses several such illustrations from ordinary life.

Finding the Lost

One example is the experience of finding that which was lost. Jesus had been associating with sinners, and the so-called respectable people were criticizing him. His response (in Luke 15) was to point out that God cared precisely for sinners, for people who were lost and needed rescuing. He told three stories—about the lost coin, the lost sheep and the lost son. In each, though, the point was the same—God's loving action to seek out and return the lost.

God, said Jesus, is like the householder who has lost a coin. She sweeps the house until she finds it, then brings in her friends to rejoice with her —"for I have found the coin which I had lost." Here the stress is on the value of what has been

45

lost without regard for responsibility. A coin, indeed, has no responsibility. It is simply lost and no effort must be spared in recovering it. Just so, while no person is like a coin, there are some who have had little control over their lives, people for whom the environment has been so harmful that they are lost in selfishness, alienated from other people, separated from their Creator. Just as the coin cannot be blamed for falling into a dark corner, some people cannot be blamed for the condition into which they fall. Yet they are lost, and they have no real future until God takes the initiative, lovingly seeks them out, picks them up and offers them renewed fellowship.

In the story of the good shepherd the primary focus remains on the eager searching of God. Even though he has a hundred sheep, when one gets lost he will take great pains to trace it down and rescue it, returning with the sheep on his shoulder and calling to his neighbors to celebrate with him. Yet the dimension of responsibility begins to emerge. The lost sheep strays from the flock and is lured farther by juicy bits of grass just beyond. Never thinking ahead, it becomes confused, loses its sense of direction and is lost. A sheep is not like a coin. There is an element of stubbornness and rebellion in its lostness. There are people like this. They are not too deeply to blame; yet they have cut themselves off from God and distorted their relations with other people. They are lost.

The return is more difficult, for unlike the

coin, the sheep must recognize his need for help; he must stop wandering and call patiently so the shepherd can find him. Similarly, the straying human being must know that he is lost and needs help. He must experience some pain of conscience, some awareness of separation, a beginning repentance before God can get through to him.

There is no more beautiful picture in the Bible than Jesus as the good shepherd. Jesus speaks of himself as the shepherd and adds, "I know my own" (John 10:14). And he says (verse 3) that the shepherd "calls his own sheep by name and leads them out."

> He leads me beside still waters;
>
> . . . .
> Even though I walk through the
>   valley of the shadow of death,
>   I fear no evil:
> for thou art with me;
>   thy rod and thy staff,
>   they comfort me (Psalm 23).

God the good shepherd cares for each individual, no matter how lost.

There is a third aspect of God's outreach. A father's younger son was impatient to receive his inheritance. When he got hold of it, he went off on his own rebelliously, and soon he had "squandered his property in loose living." This famous Prodigal Son represents the kind of responsible wrongdoing we usually think of as sin. This kind of selfish living is common enough,

47

and we easily accept it as "sowing wild oats."
Yet the results can be devastating. People who
are lost in this way take their heritage, be it
money or health or beauty or wit, and off they
go, with no restraint on their actions. The way-
ward son is more thoroughly lost than the coin
or the wandering sheep, for he is aware of, and
thus responsible for, his condition.

Of course, circumstances and events may beat
him down until he realizes his mistake. But the
return is quite difficult. Simply waiting like a
coin or calling like a sheep will not suffice. God
the loving Father is eager to help, but his loving
and seeking cannot go beyond waiting for the
prodigal's return. To do more would violate the
son's self-asserted freedom.

The rest is up to the son. If external events
do not beat him down, if he does not experience
famine and loss of friends and money, he may
remain lost a long time, even a lifetime and an
eternity. And even if circumstances do conspire
to bring him to a condition of despair, he may
not repent. He may rebel still more and turn
criminal or become a hardened cynic or commit
suicide. It's up to him.

How did the prodigal return? According to the
story, "he came to himself." He had to realize,
at least dimly, that he was destroying something
valuable, that his own person had some worth,
at least in the eyes of his father. He also had to
decide to go to his father and to confess that he
had sinned. And he did just that. It takes a sur-

render, a throwing of oneself upon the heavenly Father's mercy, before the lost can be found.

When the son approached his home, his father rushed out to greet him. He experienced his father's overflowing mercy and realized that it had always been reaching out toward him. His homecoming is one of the most poignant, richest of human happenings. It touches a chord that is nearly universal in the human breast. We can identify with the father waiting at the window and then rushing out with great joy. We can also feel a bit of the boy's inner turmoil, his transformation, his surprise and sudden warmth at the reception accorded him. The lost has been found!

Yet the story in Luke does not really end in rejoicing at all. We have yet to hear about the older brother. His lostness is particularly poignant because he never left home at all. Self-satisfied, self-righteous, "steeped in a merciless self-esteem," it did not matter what he had, for he could not receive the most precious gift of all, his father's rich love.

This is perhaps the most dangerous state of all, for it is so difficult to recognize. But its clearest warning signal is a loss of compassionate interest in those who live around us. Here is urgent warning. Reconciliation is not only the need of those who are beyond the pale of respectability. Reconciliation is the need of those who dwell at home, and who find it hard to comprehend the restlessness, the yearnings, the rejection and the violence that threaten to split our world apart. Reconciliation is needed here, but all the need is not in any one place. The son who never left home has his problems, too. He needs to see himself as part of a larger whole, as one member of a larger brotherhood that feels itself impoverished whenever any member is on the outside looking in.

His surrender must be to a Father whose love sears him, melts down the bitterness, consumes the complacency and destroys the walls of pride. God's seeking, persistent love has that kind of power. Whatever our condition of lostness, God's love pursues us. We are called to respond, and if we do, it is his love that has won us back.

The Transformation Within

The New Testament uses a number of analogies, other than the lost being found, to describe what God does for and to men through Jesus Christ. The stranger is adopted and becomes a son. Enemies are at peace through reconciliation. The accused is justified and acquitted. The unclean is washed and made clean. The debtor is forgiven his debt and set free. The slave is redeemed and set free. The dead man is given new life. The cut-off branch receives new life through engrafting. The diseased person is healed and made whole. The childish person grows into maturity. These parables of salvation range from those stressing that a new relationship is set up to those stressing that the saved person is a new

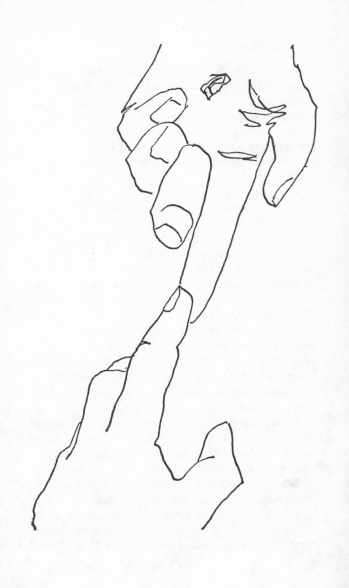

man, actually transformed within himself. In every case the New Testament puts primary emphasis on God's action, which brings something new into human life, whether it be a restoration or an entirely fresh act. The stress lies on the gospel, good news, grace (free gifts).

It was the central declaration of the New Testament that Jesus of Nazareth was the focus of God's gracious and saving action. It is the central conviction of the Christian faith that Jesus Christ continues to be that focal point. He brings new relationships, and the transformation of men takes place through his presence. He is the good news and the carrier of new life. Those who are united with him through faith are saved—reconciled and remade. Jesus Christ is both God's Word and the Christian's Lord.

In the preceding chapter we summarized human troubles with four phrases—meaningless alienation, guilt, defeat, anxiety. What God offers in Jesus Christ can be summarized in four corresponding words—fellowship, forgiveness, freedom, fulfilment.

Jesus Christ is God's Word. He is God saying the Word we long for. He is God himself come down and *into* the human condition, right beside man and identified with man in his empty living and meaningless waiting. For the isolated and alienated, this means renewed fellowship with the source, the center, the sovereign of his existence. Words are the means of communication between persons. To call Christ God's Word is to emphasize that through Christ and a man's faith in Christ the supreme person of the universe speaks to sinful men, recreating the highest reaches of their beings, renewing the divine image in them. Thus they meet once more their destiny, which is fellowship with him or participation in divine love.

Always the initiative is God's. That term "Word of God" stresses that the first decisive action in renewing the divine-human relation is God's. We are passive in receiving words. Our eyes can shift and focus, but our ears are fixed and record whatever waves come to them, often despite our efforts to attend to something else. When God chooses to speak to us, he catches and holds our attention, unless we take the decisively rebellious action of putting our hands over our ears! To say that we know God only through his Word is to point out that God is in himself very far from us, very different from us, entirely unknown and mysterious until he chooses to reveal himself to us. It is to stress the amazing fact that he *does* come to us across a great gulf. Personal communication always takes place across a gap from the mystery of one subjective self to the equal mystery of another self. From the infinite Creator to the finite creature, this self-to-self Word bridges a vast chasm indeed.

But Jesus Christ as God's Word also meets the need of the guilt ridden. A word in personal address always represents the concrete will of the speaker. Christ represents God's concrete will and decision toward every man so addressed. What he wills is forgiveness. To each he says, "For you I have a sacrificing love and I grant you the forgiveness of your sins."

The proper way for man to handle guilt feelings is to hear God's Word. This is no cheap grace, no easy Pilate-like hand washing (though Christians often seek so to abuse it). It cost the Son of God a painful death upon the cross— and it costs the recipient too, even though he cannot really pay for it. Yet to receive forgiveness from God is to have something radical happen within one. Unlike Pilate, Peter, who had denied Christ, found forgiveness through Christ and was transformed into the sturdy rock, the energetic saint who helped mightily to establish the New Testament church.

Renewed fellowship with God and forgiveness free a person to serve God and his fellowmen. To the defeated modern man the word of forgiveness means that he is set free from the tyranny of sin and the sting of death, released from the dominion of Satan and the powers of darkness upon this earth. The desperation has gone out of his search for success. He does not need to conform; he can afford to be a person. In ultimate matters he has been taken care of by God. He can relax his self-concern and give himself to serve the neighbor's need. It is not that he always succeeds but that he looks at life from a different perspective. The faith-filled Christian is possessed of a certain gay imperturbability—not irresponsible, but responsibly nonchalant.

Christian freedom does not mean lack of concern for what happens. Quite the contrary. The Christian knows that despite all appearances Christ is ultimately in control. Not only is Christ the incarnate and crucified Word, bringing fellowship, forgiveness and freedom; he is also the *resurrected Lord,* who triumphed over death and the devil. We may be frustrated and defeated in ourselves, but Christ is our Lord; he has won the victory. In fact he is Lord over this whole world, over even the powers raging against him. Christ's kingship is not yet plain and evident— it is a hidden kingdom and the king came among us incognito. We are still engaged in bitter battles, but the Christian knows where the victory lies—in his Lord Jesus Christ.

Having such a Lord not only means freedom and promised victory for defeated modern men. For anxious, diseased, unintegrated modern men, having such a Lord also means *wholeness,* salvation, health, being made a new man, a foretaste and sign of their eternal destiny with God. When a person can give himself completely to a Lord, he finds his many parts caught up in a unifying purpose, a harmonious whole—bodily drives and rhythms, spiritual aspirations and struggles all subsumed in the service of the Master. And if the Lord is also the Lord of the universe, a man will be enabled to fit into his natural and social environment, since he is aligned with reality.

But now one serious limitation must be put upon this beautiful picture of man's destiny in Christ. It is never fulfilled, never complete in this life. I believe in spiritual healing—the healing of our bodies by the experience of salvation through faith. Still this mortal flesh will die. The Christian does experience God's fellowship, freedom from anxiety, a new wholeness. In principle the victory has been won and is already ours. The curse of sin, the sting of death, the tyranny of Satan are broken. We have a foretaste of eternity. But the end is not yet. We live between the times. D-day is past; that was the first Easter: but V-day is not yet; that will be Christ's return. We are both old man and new. We remain sinners. We continue to become diseased and to die. Our struggle with Satan goes on, yet it is not meaningless. In the interim our destiny is a purpose in this life, namely, to serve God by serving our neighbors for Christ's sake.

The very shape of the cross portrays the pattern of our personal stories. Rising from its base, the lower part of the upright represents our natural life of body and spirit, moving up toward fulfilment, toward the realization of our ambitions and goals, toward richer fellowship. The crossbar cuts that off. Frustrations and failures mark our course. Our self-centered plans run into unyielding roadblocks. Events constantly confront us with threatening experiences. But life goes on beyond, a resurrected, beyond-the-cross life of faith in Christ.

Chapter Four

Word and Person

When barriers are smashed, God does the smashing. Breakthroughs are made by God. Yet since the barriers are erected by human wills and human action, God's action redirects human wills and changes human actions.

How can these things be (to repeat a question we can never quite answer)? They happen by grace and faith, by God's gracious action in Christ Jesus, which calls forth trust in those who are caught up in it and accept it. They happen when we listen to the Word of God and follow Christ as Lord.

Years ago a baby and a parakeet came into our home at about the same time. It became my habit to greet each of them: "Hi Kerry," to the bird and "Hi Melanie," to the baby.

The parakeet responded much sooner than the baby, but what a disappointing experience! What he said in return was, "Hi Kerry." I felt like telling him, "Those are my words to you, not yours to me." But of course, a bird knows nothing about a "you" or a "me." His response was not words but merely the imitation of sounds.

Though it took longer, the baby learned to respond with, "Hi Daddy." She developed more and more words as she became more and more of a self-conscious person. Words are for people.

The Person and the Word

H. H. Farmer has pointed out[1] that when we address words to another person, at least three things are involved: 1) The speech is an immediate and concrete expression of the speaker's will. 2) There is some common meaning; speaker and hearer share language and ideas, which can become the carriers of the will and intention behind the words. 3) The speech represents a claim on the one addressed, seeking his attention and response. Words are for persons, for only a person is capable of being addressed and capable of responding (he is response-able, responsible).

When we speak of the Word of God, we are emphasizing that God is a person and that he addresses each of us as a person. We are stressing that he expresses a specific will toward each of us, finds the means to announce his intention in our personal experience and confronts us to seek our personal response.

The Word of God is the gospel; it is Jesus Christ incarnate and proclaimed. The concrete will and decision of God toward every man is expressed in that supreme "event in eternity" when the Son of God became a man and lived and died and rose again for the salvation of mankind. In this act God said to each of us: "For you I have a sacrificing love and I promise you the forgiveness of sins."

But where is the shared language through which God can carry his will into human experience? He came to persons as a person. Whatever else God may be, when he reveals himself to human beings he does so as a person, as a human being. In coming into the humanity of Christ, God uses a language we can understand. We can recognize God's loving will in this man described in the gospels. That life was not only an event in eternity, but also an event in history, at a particular time and place, Palestine 2,000 years ago. That's where men find themselves—at a time and a place—so that's where God finds them with his Word. To speak of the Word of God is to point out that Christianity is an historical religion, springing from events.

Yet all this must get from "there and then" to "here and now" if it is to enter our personal experience. Within the stream of history God uses secondary carriers—not the voices of angels, not special dreams, but the speech and actions of men who proclaim Christ, written records that describe his life, water and wine and bread in sacraments that show him within the Christian fellowship. Jesus Christ is the Word; preaching, Scripture and sacraments are the chief carriers of the Word to us. Always it is personal, God in the human person of Christ expressing himself to other human persons.

It is for this reason that preaching, or proclamation, has usually had a certain priority over the Bible or over the sacraments. While proclamation has always been understood to include deeds of loving service, the emphasis on such deeds is particularly strong today. Regardless of what may or may not be expressed verbally, deeds seem to be the best way to suggest that God is here, now, as a living person and active will. In such an encounter, the human person and his immediate will are most clearly met. But how such loving deeds will convey the recognition that behind the doer stands God, saying through the deeds "I love you, John Jones," remains a problem.

But still a third step must follow. The hearer must recognize not only that God has spoken in Christ and is speaking now (in preaching, Bible reading, sacrament); the hearer must also recognize God's direct claim on his person. This is the immediate work of the Holy Spirit within a man's heart. When a person feels himself caught in his deepest personal experience, God has truly communicated his Word.

In other words, God always brings a man salvation in a double form. Christ the Word is mediated through the Bible, preaching and sacraments, a holy and loving Christian life; at the same time, the Holy Spirit acts directly on the human heart (or will). This is called mediated immediacy. God reveals himself, his love and forgiveness, immediately through the Holy Spirit and indirectly through some human carrier.

A good illustration has been suggested for what should take place every Sunday at eleven (and in all worship and prayer). Suppose you attend a Broadway play. After living through days of anticipation, struggling through traffic and finding your seat in the theater, you settle back comfortably to watch the performance. But as the lights begin to dim, a voice blares your name over the loudspeaker! "John Jones, you are wanted on the stage to take your place so that the play can begin." You are on the spot. You were observing in relaxed detachment; now you are desperately and deeply involved in the action.

Similarly, when we worship or pray or read the Bible, we are watching, we sift ideas, we judge what is going on. But when in the midst of our effort God actually speaks his Word to us, we find our whole person suddenly involved. We discover that we are being watched, that our person is being sifted, that we are judged (and forgiven and made new) by that person who is central to our existence. This does not mean that true worship is always an overwhelming emotional experience, but simply that God's Word is always deeply personal.

Freedom and the Twentieth Century

What happens to the man to whom God speaks? What does it mean to say that he is "caught in his deepest personal experience"? Does he then become the slave of a tyrant? No. Though God speaks with authority, what he says sets men free. Though Christ is Lord, allegiance to him means fulfilment. First God turns men around, and then he sets them free. First he takes them out of themselves, and then he lets them be themselves.

The real problem is to understand fully what freedom is. There has been no more stirring word in the recent centuries of Western civilization. It is not only Americans who can say with fervor, "Let music swell the breeze and ring from all the trees sweet freedom's song." Sweet freedom's song is the very theme song of our century.

Christianity has fed this flame. The coming of Jesus Christ provided fuel for the cause of freedom, but it was the reformers who raised the more explicit cry for freedom that introduced the modern age. At the Diet of Worms in 1521, Martin Luther stood before the Emperor and the Pope's representative and asserted that the massive authorities of the Middle Ages could all be wrong—popes, councils, emperors. Before the assembled dignitaries he boldly refused to repudiate what he had written, "since it is neither right nor safe to act against conscience." Here was the first great champion of modern liberty.

Of course, Luther and the other reformers did not stand alone in reaching for freedom. There were parallel movements, each seeking its own brand of liberty—capitalists striking against feudalism, peasants seeking the right to rule their own lives, nationalists repudiating the Holy Roman Empire, humanists giving free scope to their artistic spirits, explorers and scientists freely investigating the world about them. The freedom inherent in the gospel was combining with these emerging forces in northern and western Europe to produce a tradition of freedom and of free institutions that has no parallel in history—liberal democracy, economic free enterprise in an open market, a fraternal and democratic family life and a scientific method of critical experimentation.

More recent centuries have seen the theme song of freedom spread throughout the world. Not only in America was there a revolution to insure the blessings of liberty; the French had a revolution in the name of liberty, and the Russians had a different kind of revolution with the same watchword. And now a host of new nations has emerged in revolution under the banner of freedom.

Nor was revolution limited to politics. Everyone else sounded the clarion call of freedom. The philosopher extolled the rights of man; the sociologist cast off the restraints of outmoded customs and old laws; the psychologist preached sexual freedom and revolt against the age-old taboos of religion; educators polled their students on the acceptability of the Ten Commandments. In a word, the thing got out of hand. The noble bells of liberty have now become the discordant janglings of license.

You see, freedom by itself is an inadequate ideal. It's a negative concept, denoting primarily absence of limitation. Our cry has been freedom *from* this and *from* that; we have cast off restraints until the result is chaos. In the name of freedom, we have come into the midst of the many fears that make us the anxious generation.

Freedom Is Commitment

Shall we, then, abandon freedom as our ideal? No, but we must put it in its proper setting of faith or commitment. Real freedom is bound— faith-bound and conscience-bound. The free man is the one who has been seized *within*, in the deepest reaches of his spirit. That man is most free who has most committed himself to what is fundamental in his own being.

It's like the stream of water, whose freedom lies in keeping leaves and sticks from clogging it. This it can do by giving itself to its source, the spring, by welcoming the pressure that cleans and frees it, making it a stream instead of a puddle or a dry gulch.

A better illustration comes from the best in human relations—love and loyalty. What is free love? Unfortunately, the term has come to mean a restless seeking after sexual satisfaction with one partner after another. This is not free love;

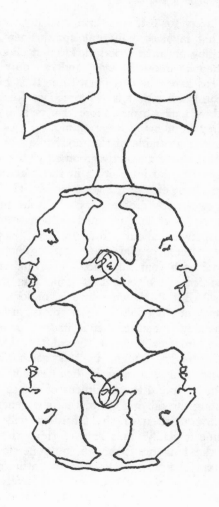

it is slavery to lust. Free love is a deep relationship that involves a lifetime commitment. It is
something given to a person. He first chooses it,
but then he is caught by it and can only affirm
what has taken hold deep within. It is binding
and constraining but is welcomed as fulfilment.
Such love makes a man more of a person; it sets
him free from many lesser things.

There is a parable of the modern age in a car-
toon that shows a smartly groomed young sophis-
ticate in her thirties visiting in the home of her
college chum of a dozen years earlier. The chum
is not so smartly dressed, has a baby in one arm
and a youngster hanging on the other, with three
more sprawled about. "But my dear," says the
visitor, "aren't you afraid of getting hopelessly
involved with your husband?" The modern generation fears involvement as something limiting
and evil. But that's what love is, or loyalty. It's
involvement that binds one's roots firmly, so
that he may find sustenance in its soil, leaving the
rest of him free to grow toward the sky.

Interestingly enough, in this generation we
are witnessing a revival of involvement as the
road to truth and the fulfilment of the self. It is
becoming the rallying cry of the new generation.
The first reaction of the Christian will be to
welcome it gladly. This kind of thing is not far
from the kingdom although, on reflection, the
Christian may wish to temper his enthusiasm as
he has in the case of freedom. Real involvement
and real freedom are found only in the setting of

ultimate faith. God made man free, but he also made him to be freely related to God. When Martin Luther spoke for freedom at the Diet of Worms, he spoke as a bound man—inwardly bound by conscience, by Scripture, by faith. "My conscience is captive to the Word of God," he declared. In a famous pamphlet he asserted that "a Christian man is the most free lord of all." Yes, but this is Christ's man, bound to Jesus Christ. He is a free lord only because he has a supreme Lord and cares about nothing else. "So if the Son makes you free, you will be free indeed" (John 8:36).

Here are the deepest reaches within a man's spirit. When faith in God grips a man there, he is truly free. Free from subservience to ecclesiastical authority, each man is enabled to exercise his own priesthood directly before God. Free from subservience to a boss or celebrity or professor or mother-in-law, free from the fear of accidents and life's calamities. Free from blind adherence to nation or race. Free from the anxious striving to please God by moral effort. Luther knew all about that: "Love God and do as you please." Above all, God-given faith frees one from the greatest tyrant of all, sin, whose throttle hold is broken by the renewal of forgiveness. By God's grace we are set free through forgiveness. We can start by asserting human freedom, but when we talk about the source of freedom, we inevitably find ourselves talking about the love of God.

Taking God at His Word

God speaks, and his Word becomes Lord for those who hear. And those who hear respond. That's what it means to be human and to be a person—to be able to respond, to be responsible. We confess our faith in him. We say yes to him. *We take him at his word!* We receive his good gifts: fellowship, forgiveness, freedom, fulfilment, and we act according to them.

Napoleon was once reviewing his troops when something frightened his horse so that it reared, threatening to throw its rider. With quick presence of mind a private stepped forward, seized the bridle and calmed the horse. "Thank you, Captain," exclaimed Napoleon. Quick as a flash the private responded: "Of what company and in what regiment, Sire?" When Napoleon had specified a vacant post, the private stepped back into the ranks a captain. He had become a captain in fact, not only because Napoleon's word had the power to make him so, but also because he had the courage to take his lord at his word.

It takes courage—plenty of it! For a private to step up and take a captain's role is risky business. For the Christian, taking his Lord at his word is a total and highly threatening decision. He is laying hold of the promise that he will be changed completely. Who in this modern world believes that people can be thoroughly changed just by accepting a new loyalty? And the wise Christian knows that there will be times when

God will seem remote; everything will go wrong and events will disprove God's promises. Yet he will remain committed to those promises, asserting that God is faithful come what may.

Of course he will waver. Of course he will warp his commitment and twist God's promises. He will rebel; or he will take satisfaction in his bold decision and the new deeds he performs. He will shape his God-given fellowship, forgiveness, freedom and fulfilment to his own style of life and the goals he sets. Like the wedding guest (Matthew 22:11–12) who refused the gift of a wedding garment (Christ's righteousness) because he was pleased with his own filthy rags of righteousness, the would-be Christian will try to get by on his own virtues and will be cast out. Naked, he will think himself quite the dandy, like the emperor who thought he was displaying rich robes before the crowd until a youngster snickered at his nakedness.

Which is he then? Is the Christian the private who acts boldly and becomes a captain, or is he the naked emperor? Both! At the same time he is saint and sinner. But his deepest commitment is to God. As long as he looks to God and clings to God's promises, he identifies himself with the saint. He can never see saintliness in himself, though others may see it and speak of his Christian virtues. Looking at himself, he can see only the sinner laid hold of by God. It is God's gracious act and man's commitment to it that defines a Christian. This double act is faith.

To Give Is to Grow

Then where are the gifts? Where is God's out-pouring love? Strangely, the Christ-committed sinner discovers resources only as he sets out to give them away. As he turns to help his neighbor, he uses strengths and skills he didn't know he had—because God's grace and good gifts are never man's to possess. He can never see them in himself; he can only see them as God's promises and as ways of helping his fellowmen.

If a man is defined by his relationships (and by his commitment to them), the Christian man is defined by his relationship/commitment to Christ and by his relationship/commitment to his needy neighbor. Because God loves us, we respond in faith and in loving service to our fellowmen. In Luther's words, "So this is now the mark by which we shall certainly know whether the birth of the Lord Christ is effective in us: If we take upon ourselves the need of our neighbor."

Is the Christian life all risk and bearing burdens and outgoing service? No, there are other experiences—peace and poise and newness. Paul's list of the fruits of the Spirit includes love, joy, peace, patience, kindness, goodness, faithfulness, gentleness and self-control (Galatians 5:22–23). These are real gifts of God, to be accepted grate-fully. When we worship God we cultivate these gifts and thank him for them. Yet they are not the fulfilment; they are flowers and fruits and refreshing fountains along the way. It is by serving his fellowmen in Christ's name that the Christian rightly receives God's grace and all good gifts. If he turns aside to possess these blessings, they shrivel and rot.

Here, then, is a corollary for our understanding of freedom. Not only is true freedom found in commitment to Jesus Christ; it is also found in commitment to one's fellowmen. Just as a person must live in human fellowship to be fully human, so he must be drawn to his neighbor in service to be fully Christian. Paul asserted (1 Corinthians 9:19): "For though I am free from all men, I have made myself a slave to all. . . ." Luther was describing the basic Christian paradox when he declared that "a Christian man is the most free lord of all." The rest of his sentence stated that the Christian "is the most dutiful servant of all." It is a fact that God-given freedom quickly binds a man to his fellows. He is gloriously set free from anxiety about himself so that he can throw himself wholeheartedly into serving those about him. "Faith," as the same reformer defined it, "is a living, daring confidence in God's grace, so sure and certain that the believer would stake his life on it a thousand times. . . . Because of it, without compulsion, a person is ready and glad to do good to everyone, to serve everyone, to suffer everything, out of love and praise to God who has shown him this grace." [2]

Chapter Five

The Matrix of Decision

Some years ago Viola Liuzzo, Detroit homemaker and mother of five, left her home to join the march from Selma to Montgomery, Alabama, in the cause of civil rights. There she was shot to death. Did she lose her life and leave her children half-orphans in response to God's will?

How does a Christian, confronted with an ethical decision, reach the course of action God would have him take? Does he use common sense; does he pray; does he follow rules from the Bible; are there binding church laws; does his conscience tell him?

The Servant Shape and the Neighbor's Need

The Christian decision is made between the two poles of the general shape of our life and the neighbor's need. In the tension between these two poles, we must reach our decision. On the one hand, there is faith; on the other, there is the proliferation of facts that describe our neighbor's need. The precise need and the particular decision depend on the situation.

First, the Christian has received the *servant shape* from Christ. The Christian's whole life is (ought to be) gospel centered; its focus is the good news of what God has done for us in Christ Jesus. Faith is the trusting reception of God and his good gifts. The rest of the Christian life is the outflow of that experience, a life of gratitude to God and loving service to fellowmen. Reconciled to God, we become reconcilers. The Christian ethic consists simply of whatever we do for Christ's sake to answer the most pressing needs of our neighbors, and our neighbors are all mankind. The formula for Christian decision is "Love God and do as you please," or better, "faith active in love" (Galatians 5:6, *New English Bible*). We are set free for others.

Not only has Christ done something crucial for us in history, dying for our salvation. He is also the pivotal point in everyone's personal story. His life is taking shape within us now. The Christian's life imitates the life of Christ—not his specific actions, his way of dress, the things he did in Galilee and in the temple, but the larger pattern, the servant shape of Christ's life. The Christian life reenacts, in endless variations, the servant shape of Christ's coming among men.[1]

73

"Therefore be imitators of God," we are exhorted in Ephesians, "as beloved children. And walk in love, as Christ loved us and gave himself up for us, a fragrant offering and sacrifice to God" (5:1–2).

Paul puts it still more aptly in Philippians 2:5–11:

> Have this mind among yourselves, which you have in Christ Jesus, who, though he was in the form of God, did not count equality with God a thing to be grasped, but emptied himself, taking the form of a servant, being born in the likeness of men. And being found in human form he humbled himself and became obedient unto death, even death on a cross. Therefore God has highly exalted him and bestowed on him the name which is above every name, that at the name of Jesus every knee should bow, in heaven and on earth and under the earth, and every tongue confess that Jesus Christ is Lord, to the glory of God the Father.

Here is the pattern, the shape of Christ's life. It shows God bending down to meet human need, the need of all men for salvation in the Son of God. We are to let our lives be shaped by the same pattern, in relation to our neighbor's need. We are to identify ourselves with our neighbor and his need, live humbly with that need, take the form of a servant in order to meet that need, suffer and in a sense die with that need and rise again with that need through Christ.

The second pole, the neighbor's need (his actual need, not the need we like to see), means that the Christian must learn the facts before he makes a decision.

Too often our discussions slip away into glowing descriptions of glittering goals or the wordy pronouncement of difficult duties. We are then left with great principles that stand far above the flow of common daily experiences. And still we do not know how to act at a given moment in a complex situation. Or we are left with rigid, outdated rules. If we apply them to the new problem, we may hurt more people than we can help.

A Christian must deal seriously with the facts. He can steer a wise course only when he has made his best effort to understand the world in which he lives, only when he has sought the most accurate analysis and full information. Christian action, of course, always takes place in a concrete situation. At the point of decision, the freedom that God's grace gives a man is the freedom to face the facts earnestly and squarely, to see the actual situation and need without bias or prejudice, without falsely tinted glasses or easy answers that have little or no relationship to the questions.

A Christian decision also involves finding God where he is already present and active. In and through this particular need and these specific facts God is at work seeking to fulfill his creative and reconciling will in these very events.

The Ethics of Response

H. Richard Niebuhr[2] has described three methods of making ethical decisions. The first is concerned primarily with the seeking of goals. It emphasizes the aspirations of human life, the tendency to reach out for fulfilment. This viewpoint considers the kingdom of God as essentially something toward which we move and for which we strive. It is the good life or the ideal society. God is one who draws us toward the goal.

A second ethical stance stresses debts, emphasizing what we owe to parents and society. The ethical person is the one who is aware of his obligations and who lives under a sense of obligation. For the Christian, the emphasis lies on what God has done for him, on his responsibilities and duties in return. Here the kingdom of God becomes primarily a realm of obedience to duties, requirements and even specific laws. If the first way tends to stress the future, this second way focuses on what has already been established.

The third viewpoint, focusing on the gospel's announcement to each person that the kingdom is now at hand, plays up the immediate dialogue or fellowship between God and man. The moral life is primarily a response to God's present activity in the world. The kingdom is the reign of the Lord now. The Christian decision and life is that which is fitting and appropriate to what God is doing in the present.

Though the first two viewpoints have some validity, the third best suits the theme of reconciliation and the ideas developed in this book. The ethic of response also fits the biblical perspective. Perhaps the most illuminating text is John 5:17: "My Father is working still, and I am working."

Christian action, then, is response to God's action in all actions upon us. Christian reconciliation is response to God's reconciling action in all that happens in the world. That is why the phrase, "go where the action is," is apt advice for the Christian. Find God at work, and rush to that spot to fit into what is happening.

This ethical position is sometimes called contextual or situation ethics, for it sees the Christian stance shaped largely by circumstances. It is more accurately termed the *ethics of response*, however, for it sees the appropriate Christian action as determined by a response to God's immediate activity in his world.

In the ethic of response the Christian faces his neighbor directly and tries to determine his need. He does not first ask, "What are my duties or my goals?" thereby erecting a grillwork of principles between himself and his neighbor. He first meets a fellowman whom he would serve. In this he also confronts his Lord and hears his Lord's call to him to be a co-worker.

The ethics of response must not be interpreted too individualistically, however. Our neighbor includes all mankind—billions of people, including those not yet born. And our God is Lord of the universe, actively at work in every bit of it, including this earth, vast constellations and mind-numbing interstellar spaces. Christian action is response to God's action in everything that happens.

We live in a universe. All things have unity, and their unity comes from the one God. Every happening, everything that is, has some of God's action in it. There may be human actions involved, but somewhere behind any happening or object God is creating and is expressing his will. What a man's body is and does, how he experiences his emotions, the thought processes of his mind—these represent God's creativity. A man's family ties, his religious associations, the way he is embedded in local and national political structures, the many voluntary associations to which he belongs, the complex system of salaries, markets and banks that sustains his economic existence, his friends and the crowds of people around him near and far—all these represent God's action when they impinge upon him. The animals, the soil and water, the sun and stars and spaces, the complex forces of nature—these too are a web that shows something about God's actions as it enfolds a man. I don't know why God made mosquitoes! To us they are pests, but God's creativity finds expression in them, and we may feel a little reluctant when we have to kill them.

All this means that we do not respond to God only in some particular religious area of life. We cannot tear the universe apart and say that God is here but not over there. We do not find him only in religious actions or in the miracles of nature or in mystical moments of awareness. God does not reserve himself only for the spiritual life, however that is defined. The Old Testament prophets, for example, saw him in the power of a pagan emperor and in the cry of the oppressed for justice.

The problem, of course, is to interpret his presence. According to the account in John 12:28–29, God the Father spoke to Jesus in a voice from heaven. The crowd that was gathered heard something. Some said it was thunder; others thought an angel had spoken; but Jesus recognized his Father. How can we recognize the action of God in any and all events?

God's Will and Ours

Clearly, we cannot receive God's will in a pure form in any one thing that happens to us. God will not constantly speak to us "out of the blue," clearly and audibly. Always human wills enter into the course of events. While that is part of God's plan, human wills also warp the whole pattern. Sin has deeply penetrated God's creation. We can see this easily when a man drinks too much and crashes his car into another, or when hatred burns in the criminal's eye. We can see it in soil erosion, polluted rivers and the nearly lethal smog that smothers cities. But this discordant note is everywhere present, even when we cannot imagine its form. The point is, the Christian is called upon to respond to what God is doing, and not to any other factor, within each event in his life.

Can we see God's will in the actions of Communists? Over the decades they have checked our inordinate pride and desire to dominate. In that way they serve God's will. Americans are far too eager to make the world safe for our brand of democracy and to Christianize the world according to our patterns of Christianity. Now Communists have thwarted this aim and therefore we must seek God's will in their actions. Equally, the Western powers have blocked Communist aspirations for world domination and have thus served as God's agents.

In any given situation we seek to respond to God and not to the sinful actions of others. The Old Testament prophets often thought of evil Babylon as God's instrument to punish Israel for her sins. This did not mean that Babylon was better than Israel, but that God used even an evil instrument to chastise his children. When Joseph's brothers stood before Joseph, who had become a great potentate in Egypt, and when they discovered that he was the brother they had long ago sold into slavery, they were very much afraid that Joseph would wreak vengeance upon them. But Joseph saw God's hand in their action. He said, "fear not . . . you meant evil against me, but God meant it for good, to bring it about that many people should be kept alive. . . ." (Genesis 50:19–20) On the cross Jesus responded not to the hatred of enemies who had pinned him there, but to the will of his Father, which also found expression there.

Furthermore, and this is very difficult, we are to respond to the God who is one. He is Creator; he is Judge; he is Reconciler. But he is also one God. We cannot say merely, here God is judging but not reconciling, or here is God's creativity but not his judgment. When a man acts like a selfish fool and suffers for it, we can easily see that God is judging, but we should also be aware that God is at the same time seeking to bring reconciliation.

The story is told of the prostitute in London on a foggy night who had the particular bad luck to accost three ministers in a row. The first one she approached was a rigid moralist, whose response was simple: "Get away from me, you breath of hell!" The second pulled his coat around him a little closer and walked by carefully on the other side, saying nothing. The third, with a deep awareness of human frailty yet with no uncertainty about his own response, tipped his hat to her and said, "Not tonight, Dearie." In any situation, we face God at work and must try to respond accordingly. I do not know how one should react in such a situation! The first minister saw only the devil at work and condemned that; the second did not know what to do because of divided feelings; the third saw a child of God. God the Creator, the Judge and the Reconciler are found in this situation, for God is one.

The Stance of Decision

Still the question persists: How do you make the Christian decision? A Detroit homemaker died in a march in Alabama. Would you ever be caught in that situation? Would it represent your true response to God's will? How would you know?

Or let's take a less dramatic situation. Several years ago I attended a retreat in Michigan. There one evening a group of us was given this fictional situation and asked to act it out in socio-drama: A man in an advertising firm in Chicago was happily situated in that city, with his children enjoying high school. But he had been told that if he wanted promotion, he should go to become the district manager in Panama. He did not want to leave Chicago, but he could not refuse advancement. Furthermore, he had been thinking about setting up his own advertising business, one of the riskiest business ventures one can enter into. How should this man decide as a Christian in this matter?

Members of the group were asked to act out two scenes: one in which the man facing this decision discussed it with his business associates and friends, and a second in which he discussed the matter at home with his wife and family. The first scene took place normally and was very well developed. But in the second scene, as this man came to talk to the person who was playing the role of his wife, he happened to mention that he

had stopped on the way home at the church and had asked God what he should do. The woman naturally asked the logical question: What did God say? The man responded that God had told him that he was to go. That settled it. There was no more for the woman or for the man to say. The scene was finished.

As one of the group discussion leaders afterward, I was quite intent on condemning that as a way of reaching Christian decisions. I described how I had just made a decision about a job offer, pointing out that I had discussed the matter carefully with my friends and family, and taken sheets of paper and written on each of them the pros and cons of both my alternatives. By this objective procedure and rational process, I tried to make up my mind what should be done. Some members of the group were shocked. They insisted that I had simply made up my own mind without asking for God's will. They went on to describe how they lived by "guidance," by asking God in prayer what to do in any given situation and then by following that decision. One woman described how she had often gone from one city to another, without any reason other than the conviction that God wanted her to do so. God, she declared, had always used her in the place where he had sent her. I in turn pointed out that they were really living only by their subjective hunches rather than by taking into consideration all the factors that God would want them to. I insisted that it was particularly unfair for that man to ask God and get his decision in a matter that very seriously involved his wife and family without having first consulted them.

This illustration points up two extremes: on the one hand, purely subjective "guidance" as a method of finding God's will; on the other, weighing all the objective factors for a rational decision. Actually, both extremes are necessary—the immediate guidance of the Holy Spirit and the mediation of God's will through the many factors in a situation, the total context surrounding a given decision.

One discerns God's will, then, by a mediated immediacy. This phrase was used in the preceding chapter to describe how God's Word comes to a man through Bible and church, preaching and sacraments and witnessing, and at the same time by the Holy Spirit speaking the saving Word directly in a person's heart. Now we are saying that God's will for Christian action is discerned in the same way. The Holy Spirit points directly to a man's best decision at the same time as the man carefully studies the facts to discover God at work.

It is in this way that a man discovers how to serve his neighbor. He is ready to serve wherever the action develops; he is prepared to be flexible in changing situations; he diagnoses the true situation and plunges in as soon as he can get a clear look at what is going on.

Does this sound difficult? The Christian decision is often quite painful, for it takes place in tension between the two poles, the servant shape and the neighbor's need. The needs of our neighbor exist in a context that may be hard to understand, but that must be explored carefully if we are to identify the places where God is at work and to heed the Spirit's prompting as to the best way to fit ourselves into God's contemporary action.

Between these poles, though, there are additional resources for Christian decision. The first is the *teamwork of the Christian community.* The Christian does not act alone. Others serve the same Lord and the same neighbor, and we are bound together in service. The emphasis is on teamwork, not on unyielding and authoritative laws that all men must obey. We are a community with a common heritage, a common goal, a common strategy. We can depend on the team, on others who are making decisions along with us. The tactics may change; immediate decisions may have to be reversed from time to time. The football team that has agreed not to pass against a certain opponent, because the opponent is too skilled at intercepting passes, may have to change its tactics radically and risk passing in the second half, when it is three touchdowns behind.

Our second resource is *perspective.* We have a heritage that gives us a vantage point for viewing our world, a way or ways of looking at contemporary needs. The Bible, church history and the history of theology—these can be rich resources for understanding the world, mankind and God's way with his world and his humanity.

When we bring these resources to bear on the context in which our neighbor's needs are set, the Holy Spirit shows us where God is acting and how we can most appropriately be part of his actions.

Chapter Six

Community Without Boundaries

Of all the analogies used to describe the life and nature of the Christian fellowship, probably none is more widely familiar than that employed by St. Paul: "Now you are the body of Christ and individually members of it." (1 Corinthians 12:27) Paul is stressing here that Christians bear a variety of gifts from the Holy Spirit and serve in differing ways, like the quite different parts of the human body that work together as a unit. The whole body could not consist of eyes or there would be no hearing. Nor can the eye say to the hand, "I have no need of you." Inferior or weaker parts of the body get just as much care as do the others. "If one member suffers, all suffer together; if one member is honored, all rejoice together." Elsewhere Paul speaks of Christ as the head and all Christians as the body, emphasizing the oneness of all Christians and their closeness to their Lord.

This organic illustration emphasizes two aspects of the Christian experience that are particularly significant today. It denies the idea that religion is a private affair—a wrongheaded notion that should have died years ago. More importantly, it stresses the indispensability of the part within the collective whole, thus providing a resource for resisting the dangerous trend toward the loss of individuality. We live in a vast impersonal world, and the modern man frequently finds himself simply a faceless number within the great organizations that shape our society—look inside a man's billfold and see what numbers label him before the state, his insurance company, his employer and so on. True membership in the Christian community is strikingly different because it is membership in a body. Each member is an organ, like the indispensably different organs of the human body.

Thus, Christians can unreservedly declare that we are in this thing together, that we are one people. The church is more than a collection of individuals who have faith in Jesus Christ. Christians are one body; they are a people of God. Using a passage in Exodus (19:1-6), the author of 1 Peter puts it like this: "But you are a chosen race, a royal priesthood, a holy nation, God's own people, that you may declare the wonderful deeds of him who called you out of darkness into his marvelous light. Once you were no people but now you are God's people." (2:9–10)

Furthermore, not only are Christians members of an organic whole, but also it is God who has created the whole, and he has done it for a purpose. He has summoned them as a task force for carrying through his mission.

It began in the Old Testament when God called the nation Israel to be his chosen people, through whom he would bring healing to the nations. After many defections and rescues, a remnant of Israel emerged as the chosen people, rather than the whole nation.

In the New Testament Jesus Christ is that remnant. He answers the call. In one sense he fulfills perfectly God's mission; in another, he simply begins the fulfilment of God's purposes and is the head of the new body that God calls for his service. All who come to faith in Christ are fitted into that body as one of the organs, as part of a whole that moves into the world to do God's reconciling work.

A New Lord, a New Spirit

How are we to describe the life of this new body that God has created for his own purposes? Ralph Morton has well described the distinctive notes found in the first decades of the life of the church.

> The first and most important note was simply *that Jesus was King of their lives.* They were no longer under subjection to the

customs of other men. They were a company of men and women who lived as Jesus had taught them to live. They lived under his rule and let his teaching order their lives.[1]

[Justin Martyr, writing in the second century, caught something of the radical implications of this new loyalty:]

"Since our persuasion by the Lord . . . we who valued above all things the acquisition of wealth and possessions now bring what we have into a common stock and communicate to everyone in need; we who hated and destroyed one another, and on account of their different manners would not share the same hearth with men of another tribe, now since the coming of Christ, live on intimate terms with them, and pray for our enemies and endeavour to persuade those who hate us to live according to the good precepts of Christ, so that they may become partakers with us of the same joyful hope." [2]

This is the note that was most striking in the consciousness of the early Christians. Their first confession, wrung from them in amazement, was: Jesus is Lord! Here was almighty God decisively touching their lives. From then on they were "in but not of the world," they thought always of one God who was beyond the world and an unseen presence in it. When they found their lives changed, their second ringing confession was: We are possessed by a new spirit! Quickly, especially with the aid of Paul's writings, they came to see that this was God's Spirit and the

Spirit of their Lord Jesus. They were keenly aware that they were reconciled to God, that they belonged to him and were his reconciling agents in the world.

Interestingly enough, what was most important to the Christians was *not* impressive to others in the Graeco-Roman world. When Christians said excitedly, We have a new Lord! His name is Jesus! their neighbors were not interested. Most men claimed some lord—human, superhuman, semidivine or a god. Quite a few people changed lords from time to time, or simply added a new one to their collection. At Athens and Rome there were many strange religions from the East, with new messiahs emerging every few years.

What was distinctive about the church from the point of view of the outside world was the transformed style of life of its members, which made itself felt in every contact between Christian and non-Christian.

For one thing, the lordship of Jesus Christ gave a new focus and unity to the life of the believer, which was noticeable to observant outsiders. The Christian had integrity; his word was good; he could be counted upon. Though he still lived with inner conflicts, he had a basis for resolving them in his new loyalty to Jesus. Quietly these humble people went about their routine tasks as men who had been set right before God and had cleared up the priorities in their own lives. These Christians were self-possessed and ready to take an interest in other people, attractive to meet and pleasant to be with. Even if one remained a stranger to their Lord Jesus and was a bit irritated by the feeling that they were not fully "of the world," one liked them and was attracted to the quality of their lives.

This new unity broke down the division between sacred and profane as decisively as did the ripping of the temple curtain when Jesus died on the cross (Mark 15:38). The lordship of Jesus Christ touched every area of human life. The earliest Christians startled their neighbors by taking this totality of commitment quite seriously. Here was a lord who really did go with his disciples into every mundane act. Everyday staple foods like bread and wine were quite able to carry the sacred presence. To scratch in the dust the simple outline of a fish was to say something secret and precious, while buying meat in the marketplace posed a question of conscience because some meat had been ceremonially dedicated to heathen gods.

This transformation of the secular and the common is seen in the symbolism of the cup. Under the spell of that symbolism, later generations of Christians would forge elaborate and elegant cups for their high altars. In the Middle Ages, the same symbol would inspire legends about a mysterious chalice, which possessed miraculous powers and was only rarely glimpsed even by the dedicated knights of Arthur's round table.

But the cup that Jesus used "on the night that

93

he was betrayed" was a common cup, to be handed round among common people. By its very ordinariness it lifted all life to a new level of meaning. The cup became a symbol of spiritual fulfilment. "My cup runneth over," we say, borrowing from the Old Testament an image that means our hearts are overflowing with gratitude because God has given us many good things. In the Garden of Gethsemane, the cup becomes a symbol of bitterness and suffering, reminding us that there is no suffering in our lives that has not been tasted to the full by the man of sorrows.

In still another vein, the cup speaks to us of the ministry of sharing. In Matthew 10:42 it is stated that the cup of cold water given out of Christian concern will have its reward. While the cup itself is not actually there in the later, vivid scene of the Last Judgment, its lengthened shadow certainly falls significantly into that picture, when those on the right hand ask: When did we give you to drink, Lord? He replies, "As you did it to one of the least of these my brethren, you did it to me" (Matthew 25:40).

The symbol of the cup pulls together the contrasts of the Christian experience—its blessings and its sorrows, its humble helpfulness and its blithe betrayals. Bane and blessing become one fabric of life. The careless shrug is forgiven and replaced with caring service. In this way ordinary things and events acquire sacred meanings and life is made whole under the lordship of Jesus Christ. Reconciled to God and to himself, the

Christian is also reconciled to the events and circumstances of the world about him. In the ancient societies this health or wholeness caught the attention of pagan neighbors.

There may be a clue for us here today. Like the age of the early church, ours is a secular age. There are religions around, but most men ignore them, take them only half seriously or relegate them to some special activity or area of life. The experiences that go between two dates on a tombstone are looked at from the flat perspective of this world alone. Such a mood may not be impressed at the outset by the proclamation of religious faith. It can scarcely ignore the presence of a vital community that approaches life with the ministry of the cup.

Boundaries Transcended

The second distinctive note of the early church, according to Morton, was its power to overcome within itself barriers of race, class and sex.

> We forget that this catholicity was not something the truth of which they learned later through hard experience. They did not learn slowly that men of other races were equally men for whom Christ had died. Rather they struggled against a conviction which they knew that Christ had spoken in their hearts. Likewise they did not come by degrees to the conclusion that women had a place with men in the church. Rather they continually tried to diminish the place that women had had in the beginning. In fact

there was almost certainly no time in the church's history when women made a greater contribution than in the first decades of the church.[3]

If Christians had been only like-minded people gathered from one class of society, they would have raised few eyebrows. But they were quite diverse, a motley crew; they were drawn from conflicting segments of society and often seemed to have nothing in common. Yet they were a tightly knit community, mixing freely across all barriers and ministering to one another without distinction. This was impressive and convincing for many observers in the ancient Roman Empire; it is convincing whenever it is encountered.

What does it mean to assert that in Christ there is neither male nor female? (Galatians 3:28) Not, of course, that Christians are a sexless breed. On the contrary, sexual differentiation is one of the most basic, all-encompassing variations among human beings (Genesis 1:27). But, under the lordship of Jesus Christ and the impact of the gospel, sexuality—like all the rest of life—is transfigured, transcended and transformed.

Sexuality is *transfigured*. The differences between male and female are illumined in a new manner, seen in a different light, viewed from a fresh perspective. What God has done in Christ makes every one of us a new person or potentially a new person, to be viewed from that standpoint. Every area of life, including the sexual, partakes of that newness.

This means that sexual differentiation is *transcended* in Christ Jesus. In Christian fellowship that distinction is no longer of driving importance. There is no inferior sex when it comes to salvation. God's grace can come equally to a man or to a woman; the overriding consideration is whether one has received God's grace or rejected it. When it comes to the kind of companionship that endures forever, because it is rooted in God, differences of male and female are overshadowed. Ultimately they do not matter.

On the other hand, sexuality is by no means eliminated. Rather it is transformed in its meaning and function. Whether one is referring to sexual relations within the marriage bond, to friendship between members of the opposite sex or to more casual social contacts, sexuality loses the warping that sin gives it when people use sex for selfish pleasure or exploitation of other people. It is returned to its original purpose—to make for heightened human community. And it receives added meaning within the common service of the church under one Lord.

Jesus treated women in the same way he treated men—as individual persons with their own particular qualities and needs. Neither in private nor in public were women considered a threat to him or his status or his reputation. From the start the church had to recognize that women could respond just as readily to God's grace and become just as effective in carrying out the church's mission as men could. Without formal arguments for equal rights for women, Christians lived such a life of love for each other that women found maturity and fulfilment in it. During the ensuing decades women received high status in Christian leadership, were among those who filled the vaguely defined office of prophet and frequently led in opening their homes as meeting places for Christians.

The church did not, it is true, set out to change the patriarchal and male-dominance patterns of their culture. In fact, even so great a Christian as the Apostle Paul was not able to rise above the tradition in which he had been reared. Succeeding generations of Christians conformed only too well to those firmly entrenched customs of their society. But the idea of spiritual equality remained, and this experience of equality before the gospel has played its part in the movement for the emancipation of women in Western civilization during the past century.

What has been said about "male and female" applies also to "Jew and Greek" and "slave and free." There were grave problems in working out relations between Jews and Gentiles within the church, but the principle was clear: "For in Christ Jesus neither circumcision nor uncircumcision is of any avail, but faith working through love" (Galatians 5:6). It is instructive to note how Paul dealt with Philemon, the Christian slave owner, when his slave, Onesimus, ran away and became a Christian, evidently under Paul's influence. Paul asked Philemon to take back his former slave "no longer as a slave but more than a slave, as a beloved brother, especially to me but how much more to you, both in the flesh and in the Lord" (Philemon 16). It is not clear whether Philemon did indeed free Onesimus. Nor did Paul suggest that slavery must be done away with. But the *meaning* of the institution of slavery was radically changed by the ties of Christian brotherhood. This barrier was *transfigured* and *transcended*. Ultimately—nearly eighteen centuries later—slavery came under concerted attack by Western Christians and was eliminated, as an institution, from our common life.

The Future Is Now

The third distinctive note of the early church was the declaration that

> . . . the church was *the foretaste of God's purpose for men.* The church was not in the world to call men to deny the world, but to call men into God's purpose for the world. The eschatological [end of the world] nature of the preaching of the early church, which sometimes makes us today think that the church was then entirely otherworldly, was the index of the church's conviction that in Christ, God's purpose for the world was going to be realized. As Irenaeus put it, the Church was "a completely new oecumenic [universal] home intended to receive the peoples of the world and guide them to their destiny beyond all the existing political orders." This new society, however small it

was, was still the earnest, the herald, and the instrument of the Divine Society which it was God's will to restore among men.[4]

This mark of the church, as the foretaste of God's purpose for men, has been the most difficult to maintain through the centuries. Yet without it the church easily becomes an exclusive club or a withdrawn, self-preoccupied sect. Without this note the church is not the church, for it does not carry through the purposes for which God sent Jesus Christ into the world. In a fundamental way the church *is* mission and exists *by* mission just as fire exists by burning. Without its outgoing, world-encompassing aspects the church is sadly perverted. As a "colony of heaven" (Philippians 3:20, Moffatt translation), Christians are a frontier settlement with responsibility to clear the way and to establish the kind of community that will point to the future. In the words of Peter, the church is the royal priesthood (1 Peter 2:9) whose responsibility is to represent the whole world before God and to bring God to the whole world.

This means evangelism on a worldwide scale, winning all men to Jesus Christ and bringing them into the Christian fellowship. The first Christian community, described ideally in Acts 2:41-47, was definitely filled with expansive power. With many ups and downs, the church throughout 2,000 years has lived under that compulsion, aware of its Master's "Go and make disciples. . . . Be my witnesses to the end of the earth" (Matthew 28:19; Acts 1:8).

101

As the foretaste of God's purpose for men, the church has had another, similar but still broader, mandate. It can be described as social action like that of leaven (Matthew 13:33), or as being "a city set on a hill" (Matthew 5:14), a sign to the nations. That is to say, the church indicates God's purposes for human society as a whole, both in itself and in its efforts within the whole human enterprise. The best single word for it is reconciliation. Perhaps the combination of peace and justice provides a good tandem definition of God's purposes for mankind as a social order (in Hebrew it is the broad *shalom*). Isaiah in a beautiful passage (11:6ff) includes the animal kingdom in this ideal order. In Colossians 1:15–20 it is asserted that in Christ are reconciled all things, indeed the whole cosmos. The note of foretaste is that broad in its implications!

What effect did this note of the church have on the pagans of the ancient world? They saw a people who were not afraid to do things differently, for instance, to pool their resources and have all things in common during the earliest years (Acts 2:44–45; 4:32). More significantly, Christians were a people possessed by hope in a day of widespread pessimism, when the society was slowly crumbling. Sometimes the Christian hope appeared entirely otherworldly, but at their best Christians asserted that Christ's return would involve not only destruction and the end of history, but also (somehow) the fulfilment of human efforts and the historical process.

Most vividly and concretely the third note made its impact like this: both Christians and outsiders viewed the church as a *dynamic movement*. Christians knew themselves to be a pilgrim people, marching toward a goal with a sense of destiny that was intended to draw along the whole of humanity. It was their Lord whom they were to meet at the end of it all. He was calling them out of their earth-bound securities, their limiting loyalties, the fortresses of old customs to which men too easily cling. They quoted the prophet Joel: "And in the last days it shall be, God declares, that I will pour out my Spirit upon all flesh" (Acts 2:17, quoting Joel 2:28). It is not surprising that Christians were characterized as "men who have turned the world upside down" (Acts 17:6). As Christians moved out from the places in which they had been secure and from the patterns of life that were familiar, they appealed to Jesus who had been put to death outside the city. He was calling them to come out. "Therefore," they said, "let us go forth to him outside the camp, bearing abuse for him. For here we have no lasting city but we seek the city which is to come" (Hebrews 13:13–14).

This strong sense of movement was often lost in later centuries. The church settled down, forged a union with the state and found its normal pattern in parishes that were firmly rooted in a geographical area and frequently limited to a religious program. The heavenly kingdom was envisioned almost entirely as being far away and beyond death. Often the influence of Christianity was used to buttress the status quo, to uphold the incumbent ruling powers and to fortify the values that seemed most important for preserving the current situation. Cathedrals pointed toward a God who was far above; they also solidly represented his blessing upon the culture of that age.

Today the society around us is changing rapidly. Things are coming loose. People are on the move —we see tiny seedbeds of ferment, sweeping campaigns for reform, excited movements of social unrest, old religions regalvanized, new sects springing up, passionate peoples reaching for nationhood, bootstrap efforts at rapid economic transformation. Any institution or group that claims to be changeless today quickly becomes a monument to the past. As someone has pointed out, today we must discern God's presence in the rapids as well as in the rocks.

Too often the church has appeared to be on the side of the established and respectable securities of any time and place. Recently, a pastor showed me around his new church building, which looked rather like a tent. I tried to compliment him by saying he seemed to have caught the spirit of the Old Testament (I could have said the spirit of the Hebrews in the New Testament) with its picture of the people of God moving through the wilderness toward a promised land. He didn't like that at all! He hadn't intended a tent but something permanent, which would invite people to find roots, the stability and security they sought.

That is simply not the church's message. The church is people who are called out. The Greek word *ecclesia*, the New Testament word for church, means "called out." Christians are people who are called out by Christ from their limited commitments, their small-circle loyalties, their trust in time-bound securities like wealth, education, health and status. Christians are those who are on the way, going somewhere, intent upon a mission and a task.

For this reason the tent, symbol of a people on the move, is a good image for the church. Abraham's call in Genesis 12:1 was this: "Go from your country and your kindred and your father's house to the land that I will show you." In Hebrews 11:8–9 it is put this way: "By faith Abraham obeyed when he was called to go out to a place which he was to receive as an inheritance; and he went out, not knowing where he was to go. By faith he sojourned in the land of promise, as in a foreign land, living in tents with Isaac and Jacob, heirs with him of the same promise."

That wasn't just a tenting trip; it was a lifetime commitment to tents and a tenting way of life. If the church is to be the foretaste of God's purpose for men, bringing God's reconciliation into this turbulent age, it will have to recover the form of a dynamic movement that casts its members into the forces that are shaping history toward new social patterns. "Let us go forth to him outside the camp . . . for we seek the city which is to come."

105

Chapter Seven

In a Revolutionary Age

"Faith working through love" (Galatians 5:6) is our formula for Christian action stemming from God's reconciling action. "Beloved, if God so loved us, we also ought to love one another" (1 John 4:11). Love does the work of reconciliation. But how can we love effectively in our huge, complexly organized modern society?

Suppose you are sightseeing on a busy street of a large city when the man in front of you stumbles or staggers and then collapses into the gutter. He needs help. How can you express love? His problem may be hunger; it may be serious illness; it may be drug addiction or excessive alcohol. You will not get far without calling specialized help— a policeman, a rescue squad, a doctor. Without large-scale institutions of health, welfare and law enforcement, your efforts to love this man would soon bog down. And you would quickly find your time, energy and money exhausted in his behalf.

In the complexities of twentieth century living, Christian love can never be simply a personal matter. For the most part, the Christian meets his neighbor not in isolation but in the context of the great social structures of our time. Most of us know nothing about the people with whom we have casual contact, brushing by them on the street or transacting business over the counter of a store. Yet we are all wrapped up in the same community; we are all responsible for developing a common life through votes and taxes, laws and customs. Christian love involves everyone in the struggle to provide social institutions that are adequate, humane and just, serving all the citizens of any community. Justice and the common welfare are the social embodiment of love.

Moreover, when one seeks justice in the impersonal structures of society he will find that there is a certain "givenness" about social life and human society. In part this givenness reflects the fact that we live within God's creation. God has so made men and so made his universe that some form of structured family life is a necessity. Men must organize to produce and consume in the economic realm. There must be some form of political activity, and there must be some common language and culture.

We must never make the mistake of supposing, however, that the institutions of our society as we now have them are what God has intended for human life. Far from it! Slums may seem as natural as swamps, but they are not. Caste systems may resemble terraced hillsides and wars seem like hurricanes, but they are in reality the creation of frail and sinful men. Many times we have confused God's order or perverted it by our own misuse. Often men have elevated the institutions of their day and treated them as sacred and unchanging. Actually, God's purposes are frequently more dynamic than we realize, pushing more for change in such areas as family life and economic patterns.

In such a world, where God governs and men keep trying to rebel, the Christian faces a double task. Recognizing that God is at work behind our social structures, creating and upholding and governing just as he does throughout his creation, the Christian out of love seeks to serve his neighbor by working for justice and the making and upholding of good laws. He may even have to use force in his office as a parent or a magistrate or a soldier (although some Christians would disagree). Part of the Christian's job as an agent of reconciliation is to help create and preserve a social order that reflects God's will. But his efforts to create such social structures may lead him into conflict with existing structures that have outlived their usefulness or have been warped out of shape by frail and sinful men. How to recognize that this point has been reached, how to support new forces which themselves are not perfect reflections of God's will, how to use power and force in such situations, above all, how to remain faithful to his task as an agent of reconciliation—these are some of the most immediate and difficult questions confronting the Christian today.

God and the Secular

There is no detailed description of the just social order in the Bible, and the social patterns reflected there do not necessarily form a basis for decision today. Our decisions in the "secular" spheres—education, politics, economics—are made without reference to supernatural powers and purposes. Here the church as an organization has no particular competence or authority. In these areas, other laws prevail, laws of growth and technical skill and human justice. And that is as it should be. The scientist, the educator, the businessman, the economist, the politician—each has his special competence and feels no need to consult religious authority.

In the Middle Ages, the church tried to dominate a whole society by providing directives for every sphere of life. In the sixteenth century, the Protestant reformers helped break this pattern, giving other segments of society their rightful independence and bringing into being what today we call secularization.

Secularization is indeed a Christian process. Its roots can be traced back to the biblical teaching that God alone is Lord, and that absolute devotion belongs to him alone. To give such devotion to

109

any lesser god—whether a state or a party or an economic ideology—is to give way to idolatry. It is to introduce the demonic into life. This can happen as readily when the church dominates life as when life is ruled by any other social institution. So the church participates gladly in the process of secularization, convinced by its history and by its faith that this is the path to social health.

Today, however, there is reason to fear that the process of secularization has gone to the extreme. Now there are large groups of people—especially industrial workers and intellectuals—who are almost entirely cut off from any religious tradition. And *secularism*, the dogmatic assertion that there is no God who has anything to do with human life and decisions, has become one of the dominant philosophies. If secularization is a healthy process, secularism is a perversion of the process. Under the guise of objectivity and self-determination, it opens the way for domination of life by unrecognized gods and by unacknowledged loyalties.

Christians need not fear a secular age. However, Christians rightly fear and seek to expose the fallacies of the virulent secularism that keeps many modern men from acquiring a mature and balanced perspective.

Christians thus approach social life with a twofold vision. They respond to the God whom they meet when they come together in worship and hear his Word expounded from the Bible. Yet they know it is the same God who is at work in all the world and in all human activity—creating, upholding, governing, judging, reconciling, guiding and serving. The whole is one close-woven pattern (though quite dimly seen). And their total lives take on one purpose—to respond to the one God by participating in all that he is doing in the world. The cup used on Sunday symbolizes all the cups of life that are in use through seven days of the week.

As Christians work within the social structures, however, they do not seek to impose dogmatic solutions. They join all kinds of people in working for justice and the common welfare, using every sort of circumstance and making common cause with all types and conditions of men. Justice and the common welfare are the immediate goals within the social struggle, though the ultimate goal—for the Christian—is always love and reconciliation before God.

To see this clearly is to understand the special ministry that is the responsibility of lay persons. It is they who are involved, experienced and trained in any particular secular sphere of life. Generally, it will be they rather than the clergy who will most effectively lead the church in its ministry to the structures and struggles of our society (or rather, in its ministry to *people* as they are caught up in the structures and struggles of our society). It will be Christian statesmen, who are wise in their field and also committed, theologically informed Christians, who can best lead the Christian church in its varied and vital political ministries.

111

Getting Down to Business

What strategies shall we use? Both good and evil are at work in the modern world. How can Christians express their loving concern and join God's action within the structures and struggles of society?

We are familiar with the long tradition that Christians express their loving concern by reaching out to help individuals in distress—those who are ill or poverty-stricken or homeless or degraded. As individual Christians and through Christian institutions, they can provide a refuge and loving care. For disadvantaged people they can seek schooling and jobs and homes. The church has always played this role. In a century that has aptly been called the Age of the Refugee, the church's personal ministry to those in need will continue to be in demand no matter how effective the welfare state becomes. There is no reason to suppose that this strategy has lost its relevance in our modern world.

Other strategies, however, are emerging. While some of them may seem strange to the Christian tradition, it must be recognized that radical change is upon us today, and that the hand of God is in it. Difficult though it may be for us to accept, the man who cries out is the man on whom the unjust structures of society bear most heavily. It is the day of revolutionaries, and—now we show our true colors—we must learn how to join them! Our best hope for a society in which men practice love and justice lies with those who foment revolution, who are turning things over and making new beginnings. God is at work provoking crisis and converting or overturning in the modern world, and we must get with it. This means we reject the call that says: Let there be peace and order; let our love first expend itself in maintaining the powers that be. Instead, we must hear and respond to the call to join the freedom fighters and the justice seekers, even though they provoke conflict and bitter struggle against the powers that be.

Across the world there is a revolution of rising expectations. People who have been mired in superstition and ignorance are stepping forward with the fierce assertion: We too are men! Men are reaching for a new dignity. As someone has put it, whole peoples are "knocking on the door of history and asking to be let in." They are "looking in the windows of the affluent societies" and deciding to get some of what they see.

The cities of North America grow and face crises, threatening an ugly octopus-like urban sprawl and calling us to create genuine human communities. Local politics—the attitudes of Christians who are voters and taxpayers—will help determine the quality of our public institutions. Will there be good libraries and schools for all residents? What quality of jails, recreational facilities and welfare institutions will we support? Will our police forces and courts know how to respond constructively to the forces of dissent, the freedom fighters and the justice seekers, and at the same time protect the public from vicious elements and wild violence? Are we ready to cultivate new moral patterns in the face of automation and decreasing employment, an economy of leisure and abundance? Christians will do much to shape or pervert, to enhance or to thwart, the revolutions all around us.

Two familiar slogans catch the idea: "Go where the action is," and "Let the world write the agenda." The crucial question then becomes: What agenda is being written for us by the Holy Spirit through current events? This is dangerous business, to be sure. In the 1930's many Germans, including many committed Christians, were sure that the God of contemporary history had raised up Adolf Hitler as a genuine savior for the German people. There are many and persuasive siren voices today seeking to lure us when we listen for the word of action from the Holy Spirit. How do we hear God's call? What is really going on?

No one can answer that question for you. You will have to do your own listening, and answering. Does no one else hear the call that seems very clear to you? But the call is for you! Does no one else respond with the answer that seems inevitable to you? But the answer must be yours. You must hear the call and join the side where you discern the better opportunity for all men to practice love and justice, where current events seem to lead to a better opportunity for a good human society under God to emerge.

The call is not always a dramatic one. Not many of us will be called to Selma for a massive demonstration. But there'll be action in our own hometown, whether it erupts in fiery cataclysm or evolves in quiet healing. Let's get with the action and commit ourselves to the cause.

Yet we are called to more than commitment to these social and political revolutions themselves. We are called to love people and seek justice within these revolutions. That gives us a slightly different perspective.

Perspective may be the most distinctive contribution we can make to revolutionary causes. Becoming involved because of our deep concern for people, we are able to contribute the perspective of that same deep concern to the activities in which we are involved. Once we find ourselves immersed in a cause, giving ourselves fully to one side in a particular struggle, we will come to know the people who are fighting that revolution. Besides many people of goodwill among our companions, we'll discover, on the one hand, some fanatics, filled with hatred or a hard ideology, and on the other hand, some cynics, intent on gaining power for themselves. We can contribute a balanced perspective, a broader look at the issues, a more realistic understanding of the meaning of what is going on.

Who is winning? Ultimately, God is. Whose day is this? Ultimately, every day is God's day; he is the creative Father, the redeeming Son and the winnowing Spirit. We know he is concerned for us, but we know he is equally concerned for our enemies. He has made us all human beings, both our enemies and ourselves, creatures bearing the dignity of his image, yet corrupted by sinful rebellion.

We cannot predict victory for our particular cause, and we are undoubtedly in for some sharp surprises as events turn. But we do know that God cares for the whole world, and we can contribute this balanced, sanity-producing, health-giving viewpoint to our fellow revolutionaries.

Deep involvement and then also *broad and high perspective.* That's a tough combination to achieve! Yet this is the contribution we can make to today's revolutionaries. God is calling his people through modern revolutions to the passionate involvement that carries with it a balanced perspective.

A Family Reunion

Our role in modern history can be pictured by imagining our life together as that of children in a large family. We have memories of happy family life together long ago; but there was a tragedy. We are orphans who were farmed out and have lived separated from one another for many years, each building up his own habits, experiences and traditions on top of the earlier common experiences. Some of us have even fought each other bitterly.

Now circumstances and our growing maturity have brought us together again. Indeed, almost strangers now, we have been *thrust* together again, reminded that we are one family and told that we must live with one another. We want to be one family, and yet we don't. Who are these others, we ask, whom we must now call brothers and sisters? And who am I? each of us asks. Do I really belong to that vague and common family tradition, or do I belong alone with my own particular experiences and my life in a foster home? Many of us remember our common father; a few of us remember an older brother who left us with a remarkable pattern for family living.

What is demanded of us—and this is God's call to us through the circumstances of contemporary events—is that we reach out to one another, seek to understand one another and work for a genuine basis for harmonious family life. The contemporary term for this is *dialogue*. By dialogue we mean a sustained talking or acting together, a serious and sensitive reaching out of person to person or group to group, an open encounter across differences in which each seeks to understand the other and is willing to be changed and shaped by what he experiences in this confrontation.

We live in one tight little world, geographically and technologically speaking, in which people with widely divergent ideas and experiences jostle each other. Radically one world, radically pluralistic. Modern humanity is thrust into synthetic and uneasy togetherness, many worlds intersecting, many values crisscrossing, many ideologies competing, many peoples mixing. As our means of communication multiply, our thought worlds divide and clash. As we approach the power of instant, worldwide coverage of an event or experience, we find it increasingly hard to say anything that will be true for all listeners or to do anything that will be understood by all observers.

This means that we must engage in dialogue just to get along with each other. We must be constantly resensitized to an awareness of other people. Where we could once assume certain relationships, we must now constantly recreate community at home, at work, at play, in the congregation.

Yet it is not a time of words alone; it is a time of deeds. Bridges between persons and between deeply divided groups can only be built by many deeds of commitment, of involvement and of service. As people act together in a common cause, they can speak in true dialogue. As one suffers for another, he can hope to communicate.

The symbol is the city—spreading, intermixing, culturally intoxicating, center of power pyramids and massive ghetto frustrations. The city is many people thrown together accidentally. It is the symbol of dialogue as both necessity and opportunity, whether through pickets and political maneuvering, or through panel discussions, articles, plays and advertisements, or through pub talk, coffee break chatter, cell groups and neighborhood child crises. In the city one engages desperately in dialogue, or he succumbs to a still more desperate loneliness; he either reaches out to others or lives in painful isolation. This is the common human condition, but it is more sharply etched in the modern city.

And here is the crucial issue the Christian brings to all our dialogue: What does it mean to be human? How can we make life together on this planet fully human? Mankind must rediscover its common humanity. We have a clue in our older brother, Jesus Christ. When we see other people, even though they are far distant from us, in the light of Christ, we know that we are all one humanity.

We shall have to listen painstakingly to people entirely different from ourselves in order to learn from them. Perhaps our first contribution to reconciliation will be change in ourselves. Take the matter of poverty and prosperity. Episcopal clergyman John Harmon, after living ten years in a Boston slum, Roxbury, says that his life in the inner city gave him a deeper understanding of an incarnational theology.[1] He admits that when he first came, he had forgotten that when Christ came among men he came "to his own home" (John 1:11). Rather, unconsciously, John went to "them" in the inner city —to ghettoed black people, dispossessed whites, impoverished slum dwellers, drunks and bums, but not "to my own people." He says he came as a romantic hero risking his life for the depressed peoples; he came as the righteous one ready to help solve the problems of those less righteous. He came as the healthy one risking infection in order to help the diseased. He came as the creative one who could provide some answers to people who were distressed and confused. He felt he knew all about such ideas as identification, availability and openness.

But he learned in the inner city that such terms belong to the people who themselves have their roots in that slum. For example, they have in their own fellowship together done much to heal the racial disease that rages in American society. John Harmon declares that his children now have a healthier outlook on life than they could have had living in a suburb. He says he found in the city grace, glory, compassion, humaneness.

As John Harmon points out, we forget that God has done something through Christ there, among those very people. He asserts that the mark of Christ is there, that Christ has made us a single new humanity. Therefore, he feels that his most important and first act is to celebrate the Eucharist, to make evident Christ's real presence there. The sickness of those people is of one piece with the sickness of the suburbs and with our own sicknesses. Our mission is simply to uncover Christ's lordship right there. The suffering of the inner city is a vicarious suffering—part of the body suffering to tell the rest of us who we are, or the world speaking the message of salvation to the "saved."

Let us enter deeply into the lives of people very different from ourselves in order to uncover Christ's lordship in those lives, in order to find evidence of the new humanity Jesus began.

The Church Renewed

Now let's take stock. These strategies—help the needy, join the revolutionaries, get into contemporary dialogues—imply something more about the church and the life of reconciliation.

For one thing, there are tensions and problems in the life of the church. How can we become revolutionaries and yet remain true to our heritage? The church is rich in tradition; can she enter into these renewing movements and still remain true to her historic self? And, if the church finds so much of her life caught up in social problems, how can she handle the controversy and conflict involved in reconciliation? How can the church keep her identity and be faithful to the truth as she knows it, if she is risking her existence in deep and frank dialogue with many other world views? How can tolerance and loyalty be wedded?

To discover these questions is to recover something we had almost forgotten about the nature of the church. Not only is it dynamic; it is also *by its very nature dialogic.* Not only is the church a pulsing movement within history; it is also a movement that seeks to engage every other movement. The church does not exist apart from the rest of humanity. It has no present life apart from what is going on in current history. To say that the church is the foretaste of God's purpose for men is not only to say something about the future of mankind; it is also to bind Christians into today's events in a way that makes their movement a dialogue with all the affairs of the world.

Such a church may frequently find itself not speaking for the community as a whole but expressing a minority point of view. If this is startling to modern Christians, it is instructive to note how many of the familiar images of the church in the New Testament—light, salt, leaven—picture her as a minority, a small part of the whole that plays a crucial role for the whole. The tiny candle in the dark room, the pinch of salt in the meat, the bit of leaven in the lump of dough— these all serve in dispersion and scattering, and just a little can go a long way. In our day too, the church must know itself as a creative minority.

The dialogic quality has been largely lost in the settled life of American Christianity. We have too narrowly limited God's Word of reconciliation to our understanding of it. We must also learn to listen to the Holy Spirit within the whole arena of human activities.

This broader view means that the church is rooted in God's creation, that one of the church's major characteristics is that it incorporates human nature. It is that part of the human race called by God to be representative of all men.

123

If we overlook this broader community we are likely to fall into the sectarian spirit, creating worshiping communities and religious groups who believe that God fulfills his significant purposes only through themselves.

This problem is most clearly visible on the overseas mission fields. In stressing the personal rather than the social dimensions of commitment to Jesus Christ, some people have too narrowly identified the true Christian convert as the one who accepts the leadership of the missionary, comes into the mission compound and lives in its institutions—sanctuary, school, hospital—entirely apart from previous associations. These mission Christians have then lived a separate existence, not interested in finding any meaning in the secular history of their people, their culture or their city.

"What the soul is in the body," the early church's *Letter to Diognetus* declared, "the Christians are in the world." This ideal, as a tension and a hope, must remain before all Christian communities today, even where they are but a tiny percentage of an essentially pagan people. At their best Christians will always try to help in shaping the formative influences in their own age and place. They will converse with the voices of the times and participate in the movements of the day. Such dialogue belongs to the nature of the church.

Chapter Eight

Barriers and Bridges

It is time now to see whether all that we have been saying about reconciliation bears any resemblance to the problems of division and tension that loom before us. To select one problem is to omit a host of others, each of which is at least as pressing. The discussion that follows is thus, in a sense, arbitrary, and it certainly does not imply that another list would not have merit. Its main intention is to select problems that seem to attract wide attention and that illustrate the complexity of the situations we face and the relevance of the understanding of Christian reconciliation at which we have arrived. These are the generation gap, situations of social tension and the need for reconciliation among differing religious faiths.

125

The Generation Gap

When a racially mixed committee of twenty students, parents and teachers met to develop a code for student dress in public schools in one Ohio city, the newspaper[1] reported:

> The chairman stated all agreed "that schools need standards for student dress and appearance."
>
> Other members "called 'outlandish hair styles' unattractive, extremist and distracting."
>
> One student said the real issue had not yet been touched, namely, "some of the natural hair styles and wild clothes that some of the Negroes wear to school."
>
> Speaking of civil liberties, one adult asserted that the committee's concern should be limited to "the area of indecent exposure." Since it is a time of changing customs, he pointed out, we should let students make up their own minds while we learn to accept variations.
>
> Immediately a woman took exception to that viewpoint and declared: "Many people of my generation are sick and tired of this so-called values gap. We support these kids and should teach them cleanliness and neatness."
>
> Students agreed that only one percent of all city students wear extremist clothes or hair styles. The adults agreed that this minority should not be forced to accept "middle class values."

The chairman concluded that this is a problem for the school principals to handle, adding that "We'll have to ride with the tide."

As Christians how can we sort out the many attitudes that make up a generation gap? On the basis of previous chapters let's agree that our commitment is to Jesus Christ, not to middle-class values, the American way of life or the customs of any one age group or period of time. We can agree that the church is (or should be) a reconciling fellowship and that it has a reconciling role to play in society. Therefore, to provide better understanding and a creative relationship between the generations is obviously one important function of Christians and the church, both within and beyond the borders of the fellowship itself.

Broadly speaking (and with many exceptions), youth are pushing for change. They give the main impetus to revolution. It is students, dropouts and exstudents all over the world who foment dissent and agitate for a reordering of society, for a political turnover. They defy established customs in dress, music, manners and the like. They strain at prevailing moral standards. They outspokenly condemn the hypocrisy they detect in older generations. Often they want responsibility, all along the line, long before the rest of society wants them to have it. Generally they are impatient with authority and tradition.

Is this the voice of the Holy Spirit? Yes, and

127

no. Surely the Holy Spirit does speak through the voices of youth today, and there is great need for more, genuine "holy impatience." But there is need for a "holy patience" as well. Christians are the bearers of a tradition and can never escape the responsibility to convey their heritage from the past to following generations. We not only listen for the Spirit's voice within contemporary events and seek sensitive, reconciling dialogue between the generations; we also transmit a tradition.

How do we go about this? First, a warning: We cannot depend on our authority to authenticate the tradition. Young people are less and less likely to accept anything simply on the say-so of their elders. We cannot hope to ram down their throats our heritage or our Christianity. We've got to be honest and open, too, because youngsters smell hypocrisy quickly these days. "The reason you can't trust anybody over thirty," declared one college girl, "is that they lie, they can't be trusted."

We shall have to interpret the tradition carefully and help oncoming generations sift the heritage. We must allow them to jettison some things that are precious to us but can only become costly baggage for their trip through life. We shall let them make their own mistakes, and we shall try to keep our own peculiarities and failures out of the way. We shall have to confess frankly, also, that we do not fully possess the heritage ourselves. We shall not say, "Since we have the light, we pass it on to you"; we shall say, "We know where there is light—let's seek it out together."

We must learn to interpret tradition as a lively resource. It offers many valuable perspectives on our present problems and our present understanding of the faith. The sharp differences between the young and the old today can be softened as both see together how varied has been the Christian tradition, how many different viewpoints have been stated and lived out by committed Christians throughout the ages. No one group or generation possesses the Christian faith in its entirety. An appeal to the church's history can reveal how many facets the tradition really has.

Too often, loyalty to tradition has meant adherence to the patterns of the last three decades in our country, our economic class, our denomination. Appeal to the entire tradition would free us all from a dogmatic appropriation of a narrow group of accepted truths and practices. On the other hand, we would also see that the new positions being espoused by fiery youngsters are not so new but also have a long history, which may help all of us see both the relevance of the long tradition of prophetic discontent and the slippery perils of irresponsible idolatry.

Our heritage, as the book of Hebrews reminds us, is a great cloud of witnesses, saints and sinners, generation upon generation confessing Christ's name. If we think of the reconciling community as only those now living, we have flattened it out inexcusably. The wisdom and experience of all the Christians of all the centuries belong in our dialogues, too.

What is true of the Christian tradition in today's tension between generations is equally true for the other traditions among us. The main line of the American tradition—revolution, liberty and justice for all—can function to unify the generations. The great worldwide human heritage (really many traditions) of the dignity of man and the unity of mankind can have a similar role. And the reconciling community of Christians should lead in the lively reinterpretation of these worthy secular traditions.

Sometimes, too, church renewal breaks out and the gospel takes a firmer grip on a new generation despite a tradition that is faltering and an older generation whose commitment is flickering. It is possible to have a Christ-created generation gap!

In thirteenth century north Italy, a wealthy merchant's son lived a frivolous life with gay companions. Calling themselves Troubadours, they would sing lustily late at night, annoying the neighbors. But Francesco Bernardone was ambitious to become a knight. He had seen a vision of swords, and one day, decked out in fine armor, he rode forth from his native town vowing that sometime he would return a great prince. Yet before he ever got into battle he took sick, became dizzy, fell from his horse and had to creep back home, depressed, humiliated and puzzled. All that happened to him while he was convalescing we do not know. But some weeks later, while still recovering, he was riding a horse when he came upon a repulsive leper. Though he had formerly been revolted by such sights, he now threw himself from his horse and embraced the man, giving him clothes and money.

Francesco had been called into thoroughgoing Christian commitment. He could have become a great knight for Christ, as some were in those days. Instead he gave himself to humbler tasks, helping beggars with gifts of clothes and money. Unfortunately, it was his father's clothing and money, and eventually his father took him into court. Francesco stood before the judge and those assembled and declared: "Up to this time I have called Pietro Bernardone my father, but now I am the servant of God." He gave his money to his father and the clothes off his back, save a loin cloth. Then, naked, penniless and alone, he went out into the cold forest, not knowing where he was to go (Hebrews 11:8). As he went he burst into song. Francis of Assisi became a Troubadour for Christ, singing songs of praise. He preached so sweetly that they say the birds stopped to listen. He preached so powerfully that whole villages were swept into his radical kind of Christianity and a great religious order sprang up in his footsteps.

Yet even this is not the full story. Francis'

radical service in Christ's name through a selfless humility and a radical freedom is not adequately symbolized by the figure of the Troubadour. When the would-be knight fell from his horse and made a fool of himself, he went all the way and became a thorough fool for Christ. And that involved a certain freedom. No longer did he live by the world's standards. He had taken on the role of those first Christians who were called men who had "turned the world upside down" (Acts 17:6). He was like a fool standing on his head! He was living by a new set of standards, free of the old limited commitments, the narrow loyalties, the fears; free for a greater commitment— to serve radically in Christ's name.

If, unaccountably, the Holy Spirit were to draw from the conventional, respectable Christians of an older generation such a brand of Christians among our own youngsters, what could we say?

A Christian Approach to Social Tension

Nowhere has it become more clear than in our national political life that our young people are reluctant to fight the battles the older generation has arranged. Though many go loyally off to war, many others refuse; they are intent on their own revolutions, even when we call them fools or put them in jail. They feel that the world they are inheriting from us is a sorry mess. And young Christians are among those who feel this most keenly.

For Americans, the war in Vietnam is both a

rough reality and a symbol of our frustration and confusion as a people. Where should national loyalty taper off into international commitment? What is it worth for the United States to achieve at least some semblance of military victory? In what ways, and to what ends, should the United States be exerting her influence around the globe? What are the basic realities in international affairs for this decade and the next? Just what is the chief enemy we face—communism, China, a population explosion, proliferation of the bomb, desperate have-not nations, nationalism itself, modern warfare itself, our own imperialism? How can we maintain and advance our own democratic political life under these pressures and other, interior ones (racism, riots, city crises)? The Christian, as a citizen and as one with a peculiar faith-commitment, is deeply involved in every one of these questions.

What is the role of the church as a reconciling community, in dealing with these urgent political issues that confront our nation? Space permits only a few pointers for thought and discussion.

First, it is important to point out that we have a theology of politics that commits the Christian church to a concern for political debate and decision. God made government. He made men as social beings who need community. This does not mean that there are not problems within our social relationships. Governing is good, but it is not the final good and it can easily go bad. Furthermore, any given regime combines good use

133

of power (for the public welfare) with misuse of power (for selfish or partisan ends).

Then what is the church's role? As an institution, it should keep some distance from the ruling regime, lest the two functions be confused or merged. For Americans this means separation of church and state, but it can never mean separation of religion and politics. The Christian's faith commitment has implications for every area of his life.

The church serves both a priestly and a prophetic function for political life. As priest, the church seeks to conserve the healthy features of the body politic, upholding good laws and orderly procedures and adding its blessing to the tasks of responsible government. As prophet the church is sharply critical where government is bad and the society has fallen into irresponsible or immoral patterns, and it works for changes that will provide more just laws and a more humane social order.

For American Christians, faith commitment means full and responsible participation in the democratic processes. Believing in good government, Christians will be active citizens—informed, eager to discuss issues, faithful in a citizen's duties as far as conscience permits, participating in a political party and willing to bear office. And the reconciling community of Christians should aggressively encourage such activities. As Christians we have a stake in maintaining, and in creating, workable democratic institutions.

Not that democracy is itself Christian or that Christians cannot live under other systems. But in North America today there is no better way to fulfill citizenship duties as Christians than to work for truly democratic processes.

Of course, democracy from the Christian perspective includes certain features that contribute to good government. It will be government by law (and a tradition of common principles, a constitution) rather than by arbitrary personal will. It will be a government of limited powers, recognizing the rights of minorities and denying that it has an aura of sacredness. It will be secular, recognizing that its citizens are under other authorities (parents, church, United Nations) and refusing to become totalitarian. It will be responsive to people who are oppressed or in special need. Finally, it will be government that takes seriously the international political machinery, that is willing to press toward a one-world political community.

The church carries out its political responsibilities through the lives of its members as they are dispersed and at work throughout the society. But the church also serves political life in more organized ways. In American denominations and congregations these ways of functioning should be greatly increased and improved—for the sake of political life and for the sake of the reconciling community itself.

For the good of both the nation and the church, we badly need study groups within congregations that deal with controversial social issues. We need to create situations where Christians can meet regularly to share their deepest convictions and work through some of their own crucial decisions in a give and take with fellow Christians. Such groups would seek to provide information and interpretation on world and national events and try to bring Christian conscience to bear on the issues. Much of our Christian fellowship should be discussing, for example, the issues of peace and war, and in particular the war in Vietnam, in ways that would inform the thinking of young men facing military service. Whenever possible such study groups should work toward a consensus on the fundamental problems and toward broad strategies for any particular issue. Then, they could follow through with some appropriate action. The main point, however, would not be a search for agreement; it would be to provide a concerned, studying, praying Christian fellowship that focuses on important political issues. In many such issues Christians will be divided about the courses of action they pursue.

What has just been stated about study groups in congregations is also true for many other groupings of Christians locally, nationally and internationally. All kinds of unofficial groups of Christians should be encouraged to gather about particular problems, for example, within a profession or an educational institution, in a peace union, a federation for civil rights, an association to support a particular political party or candidate. Sometimes these groups will want to publish statements making plain where they stand. Similarly, councils of churches and regional and national denominational organizations have a responsibility to focus Christian thinking when public opinion is divided.

When pronouncements are made by some body that assumes official status within the Christian church—a council of churches or a denomination in its national assembly—we should be careful not to claim too much authority or try to say too much. When churchmen speak as churchmen on political issues they cannot claim to represent God and 5,000 votes! But sometimes they can helpfully voice a consensus on broad social issues that will guide their fellow Christians and help to clear the air in a public debate.

Again, however, the point is not to reach consensus and accord. The point is the responsible handling of conflict. Inevitably, there will be conflict, some of it quite sharp. In our pluralistic age there are deep cleavages within society, reflecting viewpoints that are fundamentally opposed. For a healthy national life, indeed for survival, we must talk together patiently, debate the issues wisely and work our conflicts into some acceptable fabric of life. What is true on the national level is equally true, and still more urgently pressing, on the world scene. It is the search for a common humanity and a viable life together on this small planet.

This pressing need is the church's business.

The church will not die if the civilization collapses. Rather, the church is servant to the world, its peoples and its political life. Political conflicts, and all social conflicts, belong in the church —in her prayers, in her sermons and study groups and programs, in the very substance of Christian life together. Political issues that divide people may threaten to tear apart the Christian fellowship. But any Christian fellowship that tries to avoid such issues is shallow indeed. The Christian ideal of *shalom* (peace) does not mean the absence of conflict but the experience of a more basic unity in the midst of differences. Christian reconciliation does not mean the avoidance of deep differences; it means building bridges across the chasms.

At least that's the way it should be when the church is fully the church. Of course, we who make up the church are sinners and we do fail. But we try, or we are not really part of the church. And that means that all the world's conflicts should find their way into the church's discourse and celebrations, there to be healed by the reconciling community, the people of God.

When Faith Meets Faith

How, in a time of religious pluralism and diversity, can a man or a religious group take a strong stand for truth as they know it and still remain open to discuss the fundamental issues with those who differ radically? How can we combine loyalty and acceptance of differences, ad-

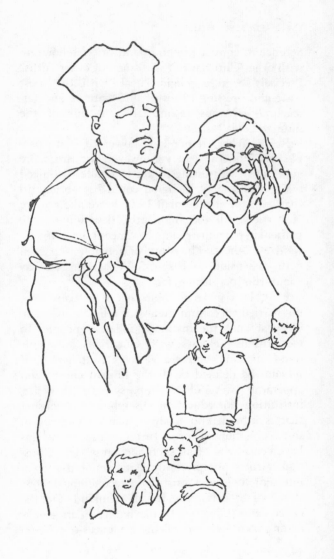

herence to correct teachings and broad fellowship with other Christians or with men of other faiths? Precisely because religion deals with the most basic and pressing issues of life, genuine and far-reaching religious reconciliation is one of the most difficult tasks.

Religion has tremendous power to unite people. In modern society, however, we are more aware of its distressing power to divide. We need one global society. Religion could be a bridge to that end; yet at present it looks more like a maze of barriers. All too frequently, devotion to one particular religious group has meant hostility toward all others. The story of religion is packed with dissension and splits. What can we say about this perplexing fact?

First, let's make it clear that Christians have no particular commitment to religion as such. They are not the distinctly religious people. In fact, rubbing elbows with Christians are many non-Christians who are at least as religious, if religion be defined as all the human energy and apparatus (ways of worship, systems of belief, institutions for education, discipline, evangelism) that is intended to relate a man to God or to some superhuman force. In one sense, Christians have been freed of all such apparatus. The Christian faith is not primarily a religion but a commitment to Jesus Christ, to a reconciling fellowship and to a purpose for all mankind. On the other hand, Christianity inevitably, in its course among men, develops all the evidences of religion and becomes one religion among many. We can try to make it a *good* religion, but this is not our central task and we may not excel at it.

Yet we are certainly concerned for reconciliation in the religious life. Committed to Jesus Christ and (secondarily but importantly) to a certain religious heritage and pattern, how do we relate to those who differ? We try hard to be fair. We give other people as much credit as we give ourselves. We recognize that other religious groups generally reach a level of sincerity equal to our own. We become adept at seeing our own shortcomings and evil with just as much horror as we view the shortcomings and evils of others.

That is, we *try* to do these things. It has not been easy in the past, and it is not easy today. But today we do have one very good pathway by which to avoid these failings—the path of dialogue. Let us meet with other religious groups and learn to know their adherents as human beings. Let us engage in dialogue with them about our deepest concerns, and eventually about the matters on which we differ. And let us, when we can agree on common goals, join hands in working to make human life more fully human for all men. This is a large job, but one that lies readily at hand for most of us.

Not that we should abandon truth as we understand it just for the sake of dialogue. Insofar as truth is built into us and defines who we are, whether based on an inherited tradition or on personal experience, we must not abandon it.

We do, however, abandon an unyielding, dogmatic grasp on truth as we understand it.

Surprisingly often, when we remain unapologetically ourselves, though open to change, we find *our* truth *in* others; we learn more about *our* truth *through* these other people; and we learn some *new* truth *from* them, even find *their* truth in ourselves. If this fails to happen, though, we express our differences without any glossing over and continue to affirm each other within the bond of humanity. We recognize that we are orphans from the same family even when we differ radically in defining that family.

The viewpoint we are expressing reflects the greatest happening in twentieth century church history—the Ecumenical Movement. After centuries in which the forces of division and separation were strong within the Christian church, creating many separate denominations and families of churches and many religious controversies within the Christian fellowship, the middle decades of the twentieth century have seen a striking and heartening reversal of the trend. The formation of the World Council of Churches in 1948 and the events of the second Vatican Council of the early 1960's were the most significant signposts. All the major families of churches and the great majority of church bodies across the world have been caught up in this sweeping movement.

The central thrust of this trend has been the deeply held conviction that, though there are serious differences among Christian groups, the unity of Christ's church should find concrete and visible expression. Christian fellowship is truncated, it is now recognized, until it directly binds together all sorts and conditions of believers. The ecumenical impulse has been a decades-long moving together of the Christian forces of the world. From the humblest occupants of pews to the churchmen with largest responsibilities, thousands upon thousands of believers have spontaneously expressed the ecumenical spirit at all levels of the church's life.

Bishops have proclaimed this movement "the great new fact of our time" and "one great ground of hope for the coming days." One woman addressed her pastor, at the close of a Roman Catholic-Lutheran service in her community: "I'd like you to meet my closest friend and neighbor. She's a Catholic and I'm Lutheran of course. We just wanted you to know how much it means to us after all these years to be able to worship together." [2]

Cleavages and tensions in the Christian fellowship remain. One of the most stubborn barriers is that which divides conservative evangelical Christians from other Christians. Conservative evangelicals tend to reject the ecumenical movement, or remain aloof. They define Christian fellowship largely in terms of those who believe as they do. Frequently, the rallying point is the literal truth of Scripture and the rejection of the so-called critical method of biblical scholarship. One earlier phase of the movement fought strenuously against the theory of biological evolution.

There are some indications that many conservative-evangelical leaders are mellowing to the point of willingness to talk with other Christians in an open spirit. And a similar process of mellowing, together with theological change and a broadening experience, have made many adherents of other traditions more willing to listen seriously. In any case, the hope of meaningful reconciliation lies in the efforts at dialogue. Let our loving fellowship be inclusive. Let us be willing to learn to know at close quarters those whose viewpoints have seemed strange or repugnant. Let our common loyalty to Christ and our common humanity make itself felt through patient dialogue.

And what about other, non-Christian religions? This is a tougher question. We can get together, dispel harmful stereotypes and find what we have in common. But we don't share Jesus Christ— or do we? Some theologians suggest that all highly developed religion in some way reflects God's pressure upon human lives. Therefore, since Jesus is God's Word and Lord of the universe, the best insights of other religions must be related in some way to God's revelation in Jesus Christ. On this basis, Christians can meet with followers of other faiths in dialogue and cooperative actions.

One special case should have particular mention—Judaism and the Jews. These people are our neighbors. There are approximately six million

Jews in North America, and Christians and Jews have shared a common history since biblical times. Tragically, it has been one of antagonism and frequent persecution, usually with the Jews as a minority suffering at the hands of Christians who predominated. Today anti-Semitism persists as a widespread prejudice among American Christians (and many others). Jews and Christians share the same Scriptures, which Christians call the Old Testament. The common Judeo-Christian tradition has had a formative influence on Western civilization. What is the task of reconciliation here?

The main need is for a deep and patient willingness to engage in dialogue, persisting beyond initial frustrations, false assumptions and blind alleys. We shall have to learn to repent and then go the second mile because of the stereotypes and prejudice handed to us by our forefathers. In the past, efforts to convert Jews have seemed to them simply the imperialistic triumphalism of Christians intent on wiping them out. Most of them are quite sensitively opposed to all efforts we may make to change them. First we must really see them, as people and neighbors. We must recognize that Judaism is a *living religion*, a vibrant resource for the faithful Jew—not just a hangover from the Old Testament or an inferior and preliminary brand of Christianity.

We have much to learn from the Jews. Their patience in suffering, for example. Even more importantly, we can learn to be a creative minority that is viewed with hostility by the majority in a society and yet makes its rich cultural contribution to the whole. Jews have not always achieved this, of course, but they have much experience and some significant successes. It will be wise for Christians to start learning how to be such a creative minority, if they are to play their servant role in the decades ahead.

Furthermore, Christians should start to realize the extent to which their faith and their tradition are bound up with Judaism. Christianity has come out of Judaism. Both Jews and Christians have heard God's call to be his covenanted people, Israel. Judaism is still trying to be faithful to that call, and St. Paul wrestled long and hard over the meaning of Jewish and Christian experience (see Romans 9–11). We Christians will learn something basic about ourselves, our own roots and the meaning of our mission to mankind, as we establish an enduring, soul-to-soul dialogue with our Jewish brothers. We can hope they will discover the riches we have found in Christ as we try to recover the full dimensions of our Jewish heritage.

Father Edward Flannery in *The Anguish of the Jews* tells this experience:

> One evening several years ago I walked north on Park Avenue in New York City in the company of a young Jewish couple. Behind us shone the huge illuminated cross the Grand Central Building displays each year at Christmas time. Glancing over her shoul-

der, the young lady—ordinarily well disposed
toward Christians—declared: "That cross
makes me shudder. It is like an evil presence." [3]

Christians cannot overnight change the impact
their own misuse of the cross has had on Jewish
consciousness. Not until they have so loved,
listened to and served their Jewish neighbors that
these people can recognize in the church a truly
reconciling fellowship will Christians be able to
speak with Jews about their most precious gift,
the crucified and risen Christ.

Chapter Nine

Salt and Leaven

Recently a group of us were discussing the question, "How do we bring reconciliation into life today?" One lady told us how she had persisted in trying to overcome the color gap by re-establishing a friendship with a black woman whom she had known ten years ago in high school. She met rebuffs and she was bewildered. We encouraged her to keep trying, but someone suggested that a more effective reconciling work for her might be to confront some of her white friends with frank questions about their racial attitudes. We couldn't promise her she would not be rebuffed.

Such a situation raises sharply the question of the role we are to play in reconciliation. What is it we are to do? What is our responsibility?

How will we know if we succeed? The Apostle Paul makes it clear that we are agents of reconciliation, but it is God in Christ who does the reconciling (2 Corinthians 5:18–19). We are called upon to be faithful and patiently persistent; we are not called upon to succeed. When we are obedient to the will of God as we have understood it, God brings his reconciling grace as he chooses, through us or without us or despite us. And men accept it or reject it. We are signs. We should be concerned about the clarity of our signal. The results are not our responsibility.

As our group explored responsibility in reconciliation further, we found that our emphasis on obedience was shifting the center of our concern. Too many of us were thinking simply in terms of finding the right way to invite people to church. There they would be subject to healing forces, and there they would become reconciled. But even this appeal is suspect for many people, and it really misses the point, besides. Our task is to make God's grace real in the flats of modern living.

Making God's Grace Real

The answer to our question is painfully simple. Though the Christian has nothing to point to, he does have a little something to give: himself in Christ. He can meet his neighbor's need in love. In any human equation he can throw himself into the balance on the side of justice and/or human need.

Not that such self-giving assures the right answer for every question. We must always remember that even in our most solemn efforts at reconciliation we may still have grasped the problem by the wrong end. As our discussion group reminded our perplexed member, in spite of her sincerity she had almost certainly been misdirecting her efforts. It is at least conceivable that she herself was unwittingly a part of the problem. Listening—patient, unremitting, humble listening—is always the first requisite if we are to make God's grace a part of our own and others' everyday lives.

Beyond this, there is always the possibility that our efforts at all-out, stark identification with the neighbor's need may be recognized as an asset by even a worldly, modern neighbor. Strangely and quietly, God moves within every conceivable kind of personal encounter to touch the lives of men.

But Christians must still learn to be content with the fact that their impact upon society will have to be more salt than sugar. It was this that Jesus asked of us, that we learn to become the salt of the earth (Matthew 5:13). We do not expect society to take on our flavor. We shall dare to hope that as scattered salt we disappear so that good-tasting, health-giving bread and meat can appear on the table. Like the leaven in the lump. Like the seed in the soil. Like dying and rising—a real dying, and a rising that takes a drastically altered form.

The Price of Reconciliation

"Unless I see in his hand the print of the nails, and place my finger in the mark of the nails, and place my hand in his side, I will not believe" (John 20:25).

Thomas' demand for specific, concrete evidence speaks for modern man. I once heard a biology professor declare that that is the kind of graduate student he is seeking. For twentieth century man any appeal to authority, to second-hand evidence, is virtually meaningless. He wants direct proof. After all, for him God is dead. In the nineteenth century the philosophers pushed God off into the outer reaches of our thought; now the scientific method has us casting nets that carefully avoid catching such a prickly fish altogether.

This means that all the old authorities are dissolving. Both physically and spiritually the fixed and majestic order of our universe has started to slip and slide, its parts moving rapidly in confusion. While our ideas of the size of the universe expand dizzyingly, psychologically the world is tightening around us and starting to squeeze and smother us. The stars that were once unalterable bodies by which men steered their course are now targets for our shots and vantage points to be possessed against our enemies.

So it is with the ancient landmarks and authorities of our social systems. "What is new in the world," says Robert Oppenheimer, "is the

151

massive character of the dissolution and corruption of authority in belief, in ritual, and in temporal order. . . ." We can no longer teach deductively, starting from the highest and broadest authoritative statement, from God's imposing revelation to certain great truths or inalienable rights to the unchanging institutions of society as the bearers of these truths. People think and live inductively today, building up their cases from many bits of concrete evidence. Uprisings, revolutions, avenues of action—why don't we try it? The older generation may cry "heresy, delinquency, Communist sympathy," but you can't stop birth pangs. Or, as C. P. Snow puts it in his novel, *The New Man*: "The party for our kind of people, for dear old western man—it's been a good party, but the host's getting impatient and it's nearly time to go." Altar and throne in Europe and in America can no longer ride high on all the currents of history.

The church as an institution has lost its hold upon the masses of people, and even upon its own members. Gone is the authority of revelation, dogma, creed, excommunication, revival emotions and ecclesiastical robes. We still have our parades in full regalia, but to most people our processionals on Sunday morning, marching into our impressive performances in our best clothes, must appear as a parade of self-righteous hypocrites, so much fraternal pageantry or playing at medieval knighthood. Our preachments carry no authority; our sacraments point to no unseen

presence; our solemn assemblies no longer startle anybody. God is dead; the church is without external authority; religion has lost its reality.

Men have lost confidence in the old bulwarks of the faith. In Nevil Shute's *On the Beach*, while massive fallout moves in upon the last continent, Australia, the Salvation Army works overtime with its revivals, under a huge banner proclaiming that there is "still time, brother." But what people really cling to as their best friend and helper is the suicide pill.

How do we show such people that God is not dead, but that his grace is at work in the twentieth century? The Christian can no longer point to authority; he can only be a man *in* Christ, a man *for* his neighbor. If he can do this, God may use him as a sign of grace.

In the end we can do no better than return to Paul's description of Jesus as one who emptied himself, took the form of a servant and became obedient unto death. Like their Lord, Christians are empty vessels that somehow pour out the treasure of God's power. The world believes that God is dead; let Christians remind men that God first became a man, and died as a man, for men.

The Christian will receive upon his bare body wounds suffered in behalf of the world. So it was with Christ. On the cross it was agony, thirst, nailprints, a swordthrust, curses and spitting. These marks of Christ's lordship among men are what alone can speak of life to modern man.

Ralph Stone has created a play called *Construction*. People from all walks of life gather on the stage of the world. They bring with them many building materials, but they don't know what to build. Finally they decide to set up a wall. Soon a visitor enters the stage and offers a blueprint for their task of construction, proposing that they build bridges instead of walls. The others crucify the newcomer.

It was in his woundprints that men of old touched the risen Christ and were assured that he had conquered death. Similarly today it will be as men see and touch wounds suffered in their behalf by Christians that they will recognize authentic life and be ready to confess the risen Christ.

> Hath he marks to lead me to him,
> If he be my guide?
> In his feet and hands are woundprints,
> And his side.[1]

Footnotes

Chapter One

1. Roy Blumhorst, *Faithful Rebels*. St. Louis: Concordia Publishing House, 1967, p. 19.
2. Carolyn T. Larson, "Strangers Can Be Friends." *The Lutheran*, August 30, 1967, p. 23.
3. Quoted from *The Natal Mercury*, August 3, 1967, by Alan Paton in *The Christian Century*, December 20, 1967, p. 1628, and excerpted from Paton's *Instrument of Thy Peace*. New York: Seabury Press, 1968.
4. *World Vision Magazine*, May, 1967.
5. Roy J. Enquist, *The Church and the University in Ferment*. Chicago: National Lutheran Council, 1965, p. 9.
6. Marilyn Plowman, "The Thermos Bottle." *The Christian Century*, October 7, 1964, p. 1232.
7. Richard J. Neuhaus, "Black Christmass." *Lutheran Forum*, December, 1967, p. 12.
8. *World Vision Magazine*, May, 1967.

Chapter Two

1. *The Nature and Destiny of Man*. London: Nisbet, 1941, I, p. 174, quoting Max Scheler.
2. *Ibid.*, p. 157.
3. *Ibid.*, p. 173.

Chapter Four

1. H. H. Farmer, *The Servant of the Word*. Philadelphia: Fortress Press, 1964.
2. Martin Luther, *Luther's Works* (American edition), Vol. 35, E. Theodore Bachmann, ed. Philadelphia: Muhlenberg Press, 1960, pp. 370–371.

Chapter Five

1. This idea is expressed and developed in *Life In Community*, Vol. III of *Christian Social Responsibility*. Philadelphia: Muhlenberg Press, 1957, Harold C. Letts, ed.
2. In the classroom lectures at Yale Divinity School.

Chapter Six

1. T. Ralph Morton, *Community of Faith*. New York: Association, 1954, p. 32.
2. *Ibid.*, p. 32, quoting *Apology of Justin Martyr*, I, 14.
3. *Ibid.*, pp. 32–33.
4. *Ibid.*, p. 34.

Chapter Seven

1. John Harmon, "The Church in the City." *Cross Currents*, Spring, 1963, pp. 149–162.

Chapter Eight

1. *Springfield Daily News* (Springfield, Ohio), August 28, 1968, pp. 1 and 14.
2. From *The Lutheran*, August 30, 1967, p. 40.
3. Edward H. Flannery, *The Anguish of the Jews*. New York; Macmillan, 1965, p. xi.

Chapter Nine

1. From the hymn, "Art Thou Weary" by John Mason Neale.

Room 753
475 Riverside Drive
New York, N. Y. 10027

Dear Reader:

Please give us your advice. We want to produce the *best books* possible for you. Give us your honest judgment about *this* book—by checking in the places on the facing page *nearest to your opinion*. Add other helpful comments.

Then tear out the page and mail it to us, at the address above. We will be grateful—and you and your fellow-readers can benefit in future books.

(see next page)

SET FREE FOR OTHERS, Frederick K. Wentz

Your age:

    under 14___ 15–24___ 25–40___ over 40___   □

I. Did you like this book?

    Great!___ liked some___ ???___ disliked___ ugh!___
                                         I. □

II. How much do you feel you learned from this book?

    A lot___ some___ a little___ nothing___ total loss___
                                         II. □

III. What difference is the book going to make in how you feel and live?

    Tremendous___ some___ at few points___ little___
    none___   III. □

IV. What effect on your views of the mission of the church?

    New zeal___ more knowhow___ more information___
    little change___ left me cold___   IV. □

V. How did this book come to you?

    Obtained from bookstore___ loaned by friend___
    church library___ text in course___ other___ (say how)
                                       V. □

VI. What changes would have made this book better for you? (Make your answer clear and simple as you can.)
                                       VI. □

Your denomination (national name) . . . .

Which of the following describes you? male___ female___

    student___ ordained___ lay person___ teacher___   □
    pupil___ education officer in local church___   □